A NEW SET OF VALUES

THE TEACHINGS OF HAFED

Communicated through Douglas Arnold

Edited and abridged by Ronald Wright

REVELATION PRESS

ISBN 0 9514038 6 9

Revelation Press
5 Mead Lane
Hertford SG13 7AG
England

Printed in England by Booksprint

This book is dedicated
to the memory of
Douglas Arnold,
who passed to spirit
on June 11th, 1994,
through whom Hafed
communicated teachings and
wisdom for almost half a century

CONTENTS

INTRODUCTION

What language can the Divine Intelligence use to explain the UNexplainable to mortal men? Particularly when their vocabulary by its very limitations make it so difficult for them to comprehend what that intelligence is trying to express.

There was a time when the human race, like all other intelligent beings throughout space, lived in a complete state of peace and harmony - showed complete obedience to the natural laws established by the Divine Creative Spirit. That time is known to humans as the 'Golden Age'.

But man grew arrogant, greedy, and instead of showing brotherly love to his neighbour, desired dominion over him, even challenging the very existence of the Divine power that had created him. Does this not sound familiar? - like a description of what is taking place in the world today? When we seek to challenge the natural laws of the universe, then ONLY destruction can result.

The Golden Age was the 'Garden of Eden' as described in the Bible, and the 'Fall from grace' of Adam and Eve (the human race), was the destruction of the world as known at that time. The people had behaved like animals, and after the destruction of their world they were reduced TO that state of being. There was however never a time when man dwelt upon the earth in the form of an ape, such as Darwin supposed, and that is why the 'missing link' has never been found nor ever will be.

Today as we are about to enter the 21st century, mankind once again stands on the threshold of total extinction - the signs are all clearly there, but short-sightedly humanity chooses to ignore them.

We live in an age of silicon chips and computers, when people are fast being replaced by machines and robots, when farm animals and poultry are regarded simply as 'products' to be experimented upon in the most diabolical way, and where nothing is natural any more - science must try to 'improve' everything.

Slowly however mankind is coming to the realisation that hand in hand with any 'improvements' to our daily lives which these scientists can offer, come a whole range of nightmare side-effects. The poisoning of crops, wildlife AND humans with chemical sprays and pesticides which also get into our water supplies, the puncturing of the ozone layer so that we are now threatened by increasing radiation from the sun and skin cancer, plus global warming which will in time raise the level of the sea and endanger low-lying lands and cities like London and Amsterdam.

Add to this the destruction of the rain forests of South America and South East Asia, the disappearance EVERY HOUR of three species of wildlife, bird or insect from the planet, together with the ever present threat of nuclear disasters like Chernobyl, and the fact that our immune systems have now become so weakened by constantly taking prescribed drugs that we face the danger of succumbing to deadlier viruses for which there is no cure, then it must become apparent to even the most simple minded among us that something NEEDS to be done, AND NOW!

But who are the people to turn to for help and guidance? Certainly not to the politicians, nor to the so-called religious leaders, some of whom, like the ex-Bishop of Durham, Dr. Jenkins, have displayed not only a total ignorance of true spiritual awareness, but even an inability to comprehend it.

The religions of the world indeed have much to answer for. All claim to have the ONLY access to God and His Truths, but in fact NONE have the answers. There is no religion in Heaven - the spirit world, and there should be no religion here on Earth, only an obedience to the laws of God the Creator, the natural laws of the universe which man is for ever trying to break down and destroy.

Something that all humans need to understand, is that after so-called 'death', we pass from this temporary material world to continue with the next stage of our existence in the world of spirit, shedding our material 'shell' in the process, in much the same way that a caterpillar sheds its casing to become a butterfly.

Here and now we are not one being, but TWO. Our bodies of flesh, the shell, being simply a mass of molecules all held in position by an invisible energy force, and IN that energy force resides our spirit counterpart - the REAL life force, the REAL us, and within that life-force resides the soul.

Only recently scientists were astonished to discover that 9/10ths of the universe is invisible. What they failed to appreciate is the LIFE, the INTELLIGENCES that live in and occupy that 'invisible' 9/10ths!

Out there IN space itself exists planets and universes beyond the imagination of our civilisation. Our most advanced scientists have barely scratched the surface of REAL knowledge. This is because their minds are restricted by their materialistic bonds, their thinking. Most of them are narrow-minded specialists, arrogant in their limited field, and contemptuous of anything outside their range. Small capacity men who have no real insight.

In the Golden Age humans did not have physical bodies. Our material 'shells' became part of our punishment after we 'fell from grace'.

The Bible stories were simply a means of illustrating to simple people certain points which the story-tellers wished to make. Jesus was always doing this, and it has always been the custom of people living in the Middle and Far East. Hence the fable of Adam and Eve.

That Divine Being which 2,000 years ago was given the name Jesus has in fact existed since the beginning of time. In the Old Testament he is frequently referred to us as 'an angel', at other times as 'a voice'. He indeed it was who gave the Ten Commandments to Moses.

Had it not been for the evil that existed in Israel 2,000 years ago, the Divine Spirit would not have felt it necessary to clothe himself also in a shell of human flesh, which although appearing to be like other men, was NOT the same. For it had those spiritual qualities which necessitated that he be born of a virgin, would later perform miracles, and, when the time came, DEMATERIALISE that earthly shell in a way that no mortal could, the 'explosion' of Christ's energy creating a lasting impression of himself on his burial cloth - the Turin Shroud.

The Divine Spirit wanted the people of earth to remain in constant contact with the far superior intelligences of the spirit world and their brothers in space, as had the prophets of old, but he also wanted to establish a set of values which would ensure that all the peoples of the world could live together in peace, harmony, and love.

Following the departure of the Divine Spirit from the earth however, and despite that fact that many thousands of people were prepared to sacrifice their lives in Roman arenas in defence of their high ideals, Rome was itself to adopt Christianity as the state religion, but by introducing its own man-made dogmas and creeds, and destroying the basic spiritual truths, it succeeded only in establishing what today has become one of the numerous religions which over the centuries have divided mankind, instead of uniting it.

Why when there is only one God, does man feel it is necessary to have so many religions? We need NONE. Only a code of LOVE by which to live by, and an obedience to the natural laws of the universe such as the Red Indians understood.

God did not cease speaking to mankind with the departure from the earth of the Divine Spirit. He has spoken since through others, but here also religious men failed to grasp the essential truths, waging 'Holy' wars against each other, more recently have come the teachings of Hafed, which you now hold in your hands.

Two thousand years ago Hafed, Arch Magus of Persia, in the company of two Zoroastrian brethren, Pacorous and Cafdraes, (not the mythological Balthasar, Melchior, and Casper), journied to Bethlehem to pay homage to the Christ-child.

As was perfectly natural and only to be expected, the three Magi who had shown such an interest in the birth of Jesus, continued to play an important role in his earthly life long afterwards, although for obvious reasons the chroniclers of the New Testament thought it wise to make no mention of this.

In the later years of his earthly life, Hafed was to travel throughout Western Europe promoting the message of the Divine Spirit, and eventually died a martyr for his faith in a Roman arena, the first in Persia.

Troubled by the fact that the pure teachings of the Divine Spirit have been contaminated over the centuries by men who wished to impose their own dogmas, creeds, and interpretations upon the people, Hafed has felt it necessary to once again champion and re-establish those truths as originally taught.

The first part of Hafed's plan was to introduce himself to the world, and this he did in 1869 in the presence of eight psychic researchers who were investigating spiritual phenomena, and through the mediumship of David Duguid, a well known Scottish medium, he began to relate details first of his earthly life 2,000 years ago, and then his experiences in the spirit world since that time.

So detailed was his account, that the investigating team were required to sit with the medium for no less than one hundred sessions over the next four years, careful notes being made of all he said, and in 1875 these notes were published as a book entitled HAFED A PRINCE OF PERSIA which immediately became a bestseller on both sides of the atlantic.

The Glasgow Christian News was to declare 'It has an interest for us greater than the contents of any other book outside the Holy Scriptures. All Christian ministers should make themselves acquainted with it'.

The Religio Philosophical Journal of Chicago, U.S.A., said 'Viewed simply as a work of the imagination, literature has nothing to equal this marvellous narrative'.

While the Spiritual Magazine of London was to state 'It is of the greatest importance - One of the most extraordinary works that has ever appeared from spirit'.

Almost a century later, in 1972, I myself became involved in a fascinating series of psychic experiences, and although I had never heard of Hafed or the existence of his autobiography, I was to become instrumental in its revival, republication in 1988, and its several reprints since then.

Later still I was to discover to my surprise, that Hafed was STILL communicating teachings and wisdom to the world, using the Harlow medium Douglas Arnold as his channel. Spirit drew us together, and I was able at times to speak directly to Hafed himself. However sadly, in June 1994 Douglas Arnold passed to spirit, but not before Hafed had made me responsible for the publication and promotion of the teachings.

Hafed's words as recorded in this book were spoken to weekly gatherings of his thirteen followers, but sadly, shortly after Douglas's passing the group split up and disbanded, leaving me with the task of raising the necessary funds to publish the teachings, in the same way that I had financed the revival of Hafed's autobiography.

Unlike the contents of the Bible which have in the past two thousand years been translated from one language to another, each version having some portions deleted, misinterpreted, or additions made to it so that what we have today is but a poor reflection of the original, A NEW SET OF VALUES has been given to mankind in the 1990s direct from one who knows Jesus well, and walked with him when the Master was a child and youth upon the earth.

So important does Hafed believe his message to be at this point in time, that he has influenced the lives of many people quite apart from David Duguid, Douglas Arnold, and myself to ensure that it should reach out to the people for whom it was intended - reach out to YOU.

Read and digest, for although the contents may seem simple, they are profound. If the human race IS to survive through the 21st century, then it is imperative that we live by A NEW SET OF VALUES.

Ronald Wright

A NEW SET OF VALUES

*

THE TEACHINGS OF HAFED

YOU ARE WORTH MORE THAN MANY SPARROWS

Can you remember the discussion we had two weeks ago, when we spoke regarding the new set of values that Jesus tried to give to those who were listening to him, talking? Can you remember what was said when he was trying to show how much God loved them? Why did we say to you that it was a new set of values that he tried to use? Why did we use that word 'values'? There was a reason why we did this.

Can I say to you that I have given this teaching, not only to those who are new here, but to others, many, many times, and they did not realise what they have, or what I have been trying to impress upon them. For what I have told you there, was one of the greater truths for you to remember.

For it was like a pin-prick in the canvas of life, letting throughout a shaft of light from the realm of spirit. It was the beginning of a new understanding. A new set of laws. A new way of valuing things.

I will tell you again, and I want you to listen. If you cannot grasp what I am saying, please say so. I will gladly expand for you what lies behind it.

Jesus said, to those who were listening, "Two sparrows are sold in a market place for a farthing, and one shall not fall from heaven, except your Heavenly Father knows it, and you are worth more than many sparrows".

I went on to say to you - why did He use this terminology, when a sparrow costs so small a sum, when dealing with people all around Him who were perhaps more materialistic in their way of life? For perhaps some listening as they were, would think to themselves, "If this is how little God loves us, He doesn't love us very much, for two sparrows in the market place cost only a farthing."

Surely it would have been better had Jesus said to them, "God loves you more than all the precious jewels and money in the king's palace." Then they, being materialistic in thought, would have said to themselves, "Well, that is a great sum indeed."

Can anybody tell me why he didn't say that to them?

The answer is: Because he had already said, "What shall it profit you to gain the whole world, and lose your very own soul?" Because the world, lock, stock and barrel, was not worth your very own soul. So how then could he compare the wealth of the world to God's love for you? He used a new set of values. He used something else which was literally priceless, and the world couldn't see it because two sparrows only cost a farthing.

He chose the life of a little sparrow, because it was divine - it was heavenly created, as all things that are divine are heavenly created. And as a sparrow is worth more than the whole world, lock, stock and barrel, that was the only way He could measure the love of God For you - By using spiritual law and not material law.

Can you understand that now? If you can't, say so.

Q: Are you saying that the sparrow is divine, and that therefore it is worth more than all the riches of the world?

A: I am indeed. I am saying that all things that God has created are priceless. Take for example a flower in that vase on the table. Where, oh where could you find me a man who could make such a flower? You could not. No way. And yet I say to you that that same flower is the thought that was in mind when He created it, as is all nature fashioned by the mind of God. The very grass beneath your feet, the trees that grow in the forest, the rivers that hold the water of life for the fish, and for all other life that lives within the rivers, because now he is using a spiritual law to measure a new value. A value that man does not have, and cannot have whilst he is here, because all other things, though they may be priceless or precious to man, they have been fashioned by man and are therefore inferior because they do not live.

Does that statuette on the table live? Can it converse with you, walk, or breathe? No, it is nothing, and though it were made of gold and set with precious stones it would have no value at all in spiritual terms. It would be worthless. It could not save your life, it cannot give you peace, it cannot give you

a moment longer on this earth than is destined to you.
Q: If all living things are precious, do we then break spiritual law by eating animals ?
A: No, because certain animals are there to serve mankind for that very purpose, and those people who talk about being vegetarians, are denying the service that those animals represent. You see there are many, many forms of life, and all of them pay tribute to God in their own way. By paying tribute to man who is the highest form of living thing throughout the entire universe, God has provided the animals in order to pay duty to man. After all is said and done, as I have just explained to you, a flower is a living thing, and a blade of grass is a living thing, so is a potato and all other things which you eat. You have no qualms about it because they do not move around on four legs, have a heart, flesh, and a body. But they still live in that way and condition that God has set for them to live.
Q: We should be concerned about the conditions that animals are kept in though, shouldn't we?
A: Always. And I do not say that all animals are there for you to enjoy eating, for there are only set animals. Horses were never intended for man to eat, neither were pigs.
Q: Pigs?
A: No, they were never intended for man to eat. Cows, and cattle of that description, sheep, fish and of course poultry are all there as food for man. If you read your scriptures, and I believe you will find it in Romans, regarding food that offends your neighbour, it will tell you there that even frogs and lizards are edible if God gives them to you to eat. For that which is unclean, God is able to make clean and edible for man. Not that I am suggesting that you go out and eat lizards and frogs. I am simply saying that this was given as an answer to those who thought that it was better not to eat food that offended their neighbour. It was stated that the food that God gives, even frogs and lizards, He can purify to be eaten by man.

Now what we have been doing, like I said, is touching upon, very, very briefly, that pin-hole in the canvas of life which allows that shaft of light to come through from the realms of spirit.

We have just barely touched upon that which is spiritual law. You will discover, as time goes by and I begin to relate all these things to each other, that the laws under which you are living are totally wrong. You will discover that the life which you have, and the way that you think and act are totally wrong. You will discover many things that you thought to be right are totally out of order. Out of step with God.

That which I have stated to you regarding Jesus speaking to the people of that time, is just simply the beginnings of that. I want to bring you to a greater and deeper concept of life itself. Of who you are, and how you are to be in order that you may be children of God.

Well you know the laws under which you live, and well you understand how those laws hold you bound as prisoners in the world in which you live. You may think to yourselves that you are free men and women, and yet none here in this world are free.

For the law that we speak of does not entail freedom, it entails injustice, it entails imprisonment, for you are all in prison yet do not realise this. You do not know it, you cannot see it, solely because it is the life that you are used to, have always lived, and know no other, but I want to turn you around and show you another way of life.

I cannot bring into this room evidence of what I say in tangible form, but I can use and apply the law of logic, common-sense and understanding. So I appeal to you in all that I say, to apply these things in order that you may find the evidence of the truth that I give you, as far fetched as it may appear to be.

I tell you that in a little while all of you will be living under this law. A law that sets you free from the daily grind that you have, the misery that you share. You might not think so, but it is so.

Do you think that God likes His children to be in prison under sets of laws like those which you live under? Well we understand why they are there, but you can remove them. You are imprisoned by your doubts and your fears are you not? You are imprisoned by your frailties, your weaknesses, your obsessions, are you not? Do those same obsessions not bring, to you a form of imprisonment which says to you - You must work each day so that you can earn enough money to pay for your existence here? To pay for your lighting, your heating, rent, and all the many other things.

But there are those who are very greedy. Greedy people who have built up empires, and they colonise you as their working ants. They do not need a prison with iron bars and barbed wire to keep you in, for you are already there. They make the laws and set the precedence for what you will earn, for what you will do, for what you will be, but I do not recall God making anybody greater than another. I do recall Him however saying, "You are my children, and you are all equal."

Who gave the world to one particular breed of man, that he should own so much land and you should be forbidden to walk upon it? You, who are equal to him, and even now more equal, because you have not set your hand against God, to shame Him in the way that they do by misusing His children, and corrupting them. His sin is the greatest, his cross is the heaviest, his guilt will surely weigh him down to the pits of hell.

Do you know where the system goes wrong? It is in their attitude towards the so-called working classes. It goes wrong because they believe they are greater than you, therefore you are inferior are you not? This is where the whole thing falls flat on its face.

Q: Are you proposing that the whole of the lands be divided up equally, and we should go back to the land?

A: No, I am not proposing anything. It is like I said earlier to you, the things that I will bring to you, you will find it difficult to believe.

Let us move on from here. Having shown you the kind of injustice that is in the world, but in no way suggesting that there should be a sudden shareout because this would be equally wrong, can you recall what Jesus said prior to saying about the sparrows in the market place? Can you remember how it began? Before he spoke to the crowd to explain how much God loved them, what did he say to them?

He spoke about why you are too concerned with what you should eat, what you should drink, and where you will live. For your Heavenly Father knows you have need of all these things, and He will provide them. Do you remember that being said in the scriptures? Why is it then that you do not have Faith in His words? Do you think He would not do it?

He would do it, but you consider He would take too long. You are so impatient. But you see, there is no way God can fulfil that promise while man is living under carnal law. For we are talking about spiritual law, are we not?

So then, I must also remind you that after Jesus said "Your Heavenly Father knows you have need of all these things, and He will supply them", he also said "But seek ye first the kingdom of heaven, and all these things shall be added unto you", something man fails to hear.

Why do you think he said "Seek ye first the kingdom of heaven"? Simply because that is the only way that you can live under spiritual law. Consider Him who is Lord of all. Who is, in spiritual wealth, light years away from you, and yet is your brother. Consider Him.

For here was He, the only Son of God, here on earth, and He lived under spiritual law. He didn't live under carnal law, but under spiritual law. The evidence of what He said about God supplying mans' needs, He clearly demonstrated by feeding the five thousand with a few loaves and fishes, did He not? He walked upon the water. He forbade the storm - told it to cease and it obeyed Him. Raised the dead and healed the sick like none other had. BECAUSE HE WAS LIVING UNDER SPIRITUAL LAW.

So, then, it is the same for YOU when you live under spiritual law. When you, as you are now, seek ye first the kingdom of heaven.

What of Moses, when he travelled through the wilderness with the Jewish nation that had just come from Egypt? Who fed them if it was not, God? He supplied their food just as He would for you.

There have been people born - masters you might call them, born here in this world since the time of Christ, who have been able to pluck fruit from trees which did not normally bear that type of fruit, and also pluck it out of season, and there are many hundreds of people who bore witness to it happening, but you do not know of it because your television would sooner provide you with a diet of sex and violence, rather than give you the truth.

So we begin to see something of the new set of values that I spoke of. Do these values go to make the spiritual law? That is the very law itself.

You see, those who live under carnal law, have need, because they do not follow spiritual law, but spiritual law is automatically in operation. For example, if you lived under spiritual law, you would no more think of going into a public house and getting yourself drunk, than you would of throwing yourself into a fire, because spiritual law would dictate within you that this was wrong. For God did no give you free will that you lose it by becoming a victim of drunkenness. Do you understand me? And this is part of the make-up and fabric of the world of entertainment in which you live.

Morality, sexual morality, is another which is totally out of step. It is, in effect, part of pollution. For it is polluting your body. Creating a child of sin. I know sin is an old fashioned word, is it not? But you cannot change the truth, regardless of what word you call it, it is the same, and the same results are in evidence. Just as surely as if you drink too much you will become drunk, so then, if you commit these offences against your physical body and the law of life, then the same thing will happen. It is inevitable, because that is the only way you can go. It is as simple as that.

That is what I mean when I say I wish you to apply your logic and your commonsense. You see, what you do not realise are the conditions which you create in a spiritual way, for by giving yourself up to drink, is also to encourage the influence of the lower forces, the forces of darkness that control you. Many an act of sin is committed in that state of being.

Q: You don't mean drinking full stop?
A: Full stop.
Q: You mean any kind of drink, wine...?
A: I mean any kind of alcoholic drink that will rob you of your mind. Would you consider that to be right? Well I understand that you may see it as a means of entertainment, but I have just said to you, before we are finished we are going to turn the world upside down.
Q: So, are you saying no drink at all?
A: None whatsoever. You cannot live on the fence. You cannot dwell in the devil's house and hope to walk in God's garden.
Q: In the Bible wine is consumed.
A: Wine is consumed, but if you read the Bible, you will find many reports where God said that alcohol is wrong. That man infumes himself with drunkenness.
Q: So it is a process which man has used the fruits of the earth to make a substance which is not.
A: Yes.
Q: So why did Jesus turn water into wine?
A: He did this because of a man and the wedding that He was attending. It represented the way in which they lived. How could He stop and try to tell them any different? He could not.

It was like the ten commandments that were given to Moses. Think about that. They were NOT THE ORIGINAL ONES, but they had been watered down, because man could never have lived by the original ones.

Think about alcohol - a means of obsession, and we are looking towards the law of freedom because the law IS freedom. How do you overcome that? Do you think that by simply making the change called death, it will alter things?

If you desire a drink now, and that form of entertainment, you will not alter when you make the change called death. You will be the same. So, sooner or later, you have got to face up to the truth that you cannot continue like this. It is not the law of God.
Q: What about smoking?

A: Smoking is wrong! I have said this many, many times. It inflicts disease on both the body and the mind.

Do you remember the first time we came together, and I told you about these things and the goals that you must aim for? I told you that you might not succeed, and though you try and try again, you will be knocked down, but as long as you are prepared to pick yourself up and continue on, that is all that is asked of you, because you are living under carnal law.

If you want the truth, I will give you the truth but I cannot hide the facts from you. If it happens not to coincide with the way you think or live your life, I am sorry, but I must give you the truth. If I do not do this, I am failing in my duty towards you. For when you make the change called death and come face to face with me, you will say, "Why did you not tell me that I was doing wrong? Now I have it to overcome here, and it is far harder here to overcome this problem". And so it is!

Q: Can you use alcohol in cooking, or should you not consume it in any form at all?

A: I cannot be your judge about what you should do. I have told you that alcohol is not acceptable. No more than adultery is acceptable, or lust is acceptable, for all these things are inflicting a disease upon you. A disease that will eventually bring you to the darkness. The dark side of your nature, this is what you give vent to. Not the God man within you, but the dark side of your nature.

You see, it is the whole way your life is conducted here on earth that you will find difficult to accept and see as being acceptable. You might say we lead a very boring type of existence when we make the change called death - you cannot do this, and you cannot do that. This is wrong, and that is wrong. What DO you do all day? But you say this only out of ignorance, not out of knowledge, because you have never lived any other way. Until you do, you cannot know what pleasures there are to be lived under spiritual law. Far greater than anything you can possibly imagine at the moment. You may have all your technical marvels, but do they make you any happier? Any more contented? Are you at peace with yourself? Do you

have that inner joy within you?
A: No. It is escapism.
Hafed: That's right. That is exactly what it is.

I want to bring you now to the very perimeter of that new concept of life that I am asking you to not only look upon, but share with us. For I tell you that as Jesus lived in that light under spiritual law, so can you. If your aim is true - that is what you have to be, true to God, and yourself, then I will reveal to you, the way that we go from here. Little by little, I will refer back to the world in which you live, and show you the two comparisons so that you may make your own judgement according to your commonsense and your logic, then move on.

The kingdom of heaven, it knows no end, just as the kingdom of the universe knows no end. Do not confuse the two as being one, for they are two separate things, two separate kingdoms, but all is God's kingdom.

I will show you how that new law, by which you live, will set you free. Free from the chains that bind you to earth. Free to go forth and use your own mind and your own time as you will, to discover the things that you want to know. For in this world is the greatest challenge of all time.

You will begin a journey of adventure that you could not possibly begin to dream of, and that is the kind of freedom that I speak to you of. Where there are none to tell you "You cannot go there, you have got to go here. You have got to do this and that" as you have now.

Where you are your own person, and we can come together in that newness of life, as you do here in this sanctuary, when we sit and talk, you and I, face to face, about the many great and wonderful things that are possible, and we can enjoy the pleasures of each others company, and share our lives with each other, in a way that other people on Earth are unable to at present.

I will unravel the gifts of spirit for you, and show you how to use them, so that with the power of your imagination, you can travel where you will. Either forwards or backwards in time, or across space to other planets. Or deeper into the spirit world.

I can show you a new way of life that has nothing but peace and joy within it. Where you have no need to rest, for you have no body to grow weary, and always you are feeling filled with the energy of life.

You will have no need to eat or to drink, since there is nothing to sustain and keep alive, and where you may journey with your friends wherever you wish to go - here on earth, on planets across the universe, or even deeper into the heavens above.

You can revisit times in history where and when great moments have taken place - even hear Jesus giving His sermon on the mount, and listen to every word, for He did not say in vain "There are those here who shall not taste of death until they see me coming again in all my glory." All those who stood around Him then in the physical body, are dead, have travelled on. So to whom was He referring, if it wasn't to those yet to be born?

Do you understand what I mean? If you don't, say so!

Q: Could you repeat what Jesus said?

A: Jesus said, "There are those standing here now, who will not taste death until they see me come again in all my glory."

Now all those who were around Him in their physical bodies passed to spirit. He was not addressing them, but referring to the unborn - those many bright souls in the world of spirit that were yet to be born on earth, and would not be born for many, many years, who tended the needs of Jesus when He was here in the flesh. That time is coming full circle. Those same people will be born, and will not die until they see Him come for the second time.

Do you see? Do you understand me now? This is what I mean when I say that by the power of spirit and by the imagination that is invested in you by God, if only you knew how to use it correctly, you will, in time, be able to go back and revisit any moment in history. You could possibly go back and listen again to Him saying those same words, for nothing is ever lost. All is contained within the vibrations of time.

You will use that gift to go back into your own lives and unravel the bitter disappointments that you had, and learn why you experienced them, because you will need to know before you can go on in progression. Only by going back and revisiting that time will you be able to see both sides of the story. Not just yours, but others who were locked with you in that experience. Out of it, you will find the answer that you could not discover while you were here. Do you understand me? Is there anyone who does not understand me?

Q: You will show us in the next few weeks how we can do that?

A: No I will not, and I never said I would. What I said was, "There will come a time when you will live under spiritual law, and I will be able to show you how, through the power of your mind, you can transport yourself from one place to another at the speed of thought, which is faster than light. So do you understand what I mean now?

Q: How far away is that time? Is it while we are in the body?

A: It is in no moment at all as I am, many years as you are. It is how you measure time, and time doesn't govern me as it governs you. On earth you count the seconds, the minutes, and the hours, for people buy these from you, do they not? With me, there is no time. No such thing as time. It could be for me a moment away, but for you, many years,

Q: Will this be after the second coming, when this time will prevail?

A: Patience my son.

With those words I leave you, and take my leave until we meet again. Loving Father, as we come to the close of this day, and ask you to place in our minds, in order of value, all the things that we have need to learn and remember, so as to live day by day, give us a deeper concept of life in which we live. Show us how to be graceful, gentle, kind. How to see all men not only as equal, but as our brothers, and love them with that quality of love that we often reserve only for our loved ones. Bring us closer to the animal kingdom, dear Father. Let us see their grace and their strength and their beauty. Make us more wise in how to help them live a fuller and better life. Let the spirit of understanding be with us, and teach us about Mother Nature and what she has to learn us. The wonders of her plants and her trees, and how we can make better people through understanding the forces of that law.

Make us mindful of the needs of little children. Teach us ever to love then and care for them, whether they are ours or not. For they are indeed the younger members of your family. We should all be grateful for the knowledge that we participate in that wonderful family.

Share with us the gifts of the spirit, Father. Your spirit, your secrets, that you will interpret for us the truth, in life. Let us drink from the waters of life, and be ever mindful, Father, of whence they came.

All these things dear Father, we do ask in that most noble name of Jesus Christ, Thy Son, our Lord and Comforter. Amen.

And so the journey of life goes forward my children, and takes us to another place along the road, when we shall assemble together. Take home with you the thoughts that have been imparted to you. Do not lose them, for what you are losing is a greater treasure than anything you possess in this world. It is priceless.

Do not easily forget the things I have told you to remember, for they too are priceless. If ever you want that crown of life to shine upon your head in all its radiance, beauty and splendour, then you must be diligent to these things that I have told you. You must be humble to your Heavenly Father.

Goodnight and God bless each one of you.

YOU ARE YOUR BROTHER'S KEEPER

God bless you my children. You have a very glorious day today, have you not? Another miracle of God. Another way of saying to His children that He loves them, and this is the way their lives should be. Not in torment, not in fear, not with hatred and violence, but a great calm and beauty in the warmth of the sun, that your souls may be nourished in the Godly things of life.

My children, I would wish for you this day, before we begin, to sit quietly and think about those who are in such terrible torment. Those who are Kurds, thousands and thousands who have nothing, and even that which they do have - their very lives are being taken from them. No-one should live in such terror, no-one should be put to such anguish, such utter desolation. I want you to go into that silence, and ask your God for His help for them.

Thank you my children.

What would you think is the duty of parents towards their children? Would anybody like to say? Some of you are parents yourselves.

A: To guide them with love.

Hafed: Yes, quite so.

A: To care for them.

Hafed: Yes. What else?

A: To teach them all the spiritual values that we hold ourselves.

Hafed: Yes.

A: To give them enough freedom to make their own mistakes, and yet be able to come back for guidance.

Hafed: Yes.

A: To be prepared to help, and to care for other people.

A: To be a good example to them.

A: To discipline them.

Hafed: You would say then, that basically the duty of a parent is to instill within them all those qualities that you know to be right.

The duty of a parent is to protect and provide for their children, is it not?
A: Yes, Until they reach a certain age, and then they have to do it themselves, standing on their own two feet.
Hafed: Would you consider then, that you are of that age where you no longer need the guidance and protection of your father?
A: Oh no, you always need it, but you have also got to learn to live without it at times. You always need protection, love and understanding, no matter how old you are, and are we talking about our own children or other peoples?
Hafed: We are talking here as parents of your own children, remembering that you are a child of God. Whatever is your duty towards your children, has to be the duty of God towards you, for it is the same law that He, like you, protects and provides for His children.

As well you know, as your children grow older they become wayward, and will not take advise from their parents - will not see the logic in their parents advice. Because they do this, their parents turn away from them, for you cannot help those who will not take help, who do not believe they need help. You can only help those who ask for help, and if you look at your world you can see exactly what has happened, inasmuch as there are those who walk the streets and live in the streets even though they have homes to go to.

It may be that their parents have cast them aside and will have nothing more to do with them, in which case they have failed in their duty towards their own. It may well be that the children have turned away from their parents and become violent. Have become filled with a need for the bright lights of life, drugs, gambling, and a variety of many other things that guide their feet down hill, not up, into that pit of misery at the end of their road.

The parents can no more do anything about that than God can do about those of His sons and daughters who turn away and will not heed His advise, even though that advise has always been good advise, has always held and led them to happiness. The joy of living is in the seed of wisdom that God will give. He upholds His duty towards those of His children who will heed His words, and who will listen and follow His ways.

If you look at this and see it as being a law, a spiritual law, then you will see why it is also written 'Seek ye first the kingdom of heaven', for that is the throne of your God. That is to say, that you will follow Him, that you will allow His will to be done in and through you, and that will is the will of love which, when placed in your life becomes the crown jewels that can motivate you to the very heights of spiritual understanding.

We speak about faith here, we speak about love, but we have no way of measuring any of these things to see what depth they go within you. It may well be that fear, faith and love are all in you, but to what degree? Whatever degree of love is in you, the rest is made up of faith and fear.

Man always fears the unknown. If we say then, that the dutiful parents must give protection, and must give love and guidance, must fulfil all these obligations, then the same applies to God. This is a God that is unseen by you. This is a God that is heresay. This is not a God who comes like a father comes to his children and speaks openly with them. It is a God whereby faith communicates between you and Him. It is a God who instills within the spiritual mind, the law, the will, of love.

He speaks without words. He speaks by feeling, by caring. He gives you a sense of knowing and an acute awareness of what is right. If God then will protect and provide for you, as is His duty, the one thing that stands between that happening is your faith in your God and the fear that is in you which says, "Will He do it though? Will He be my protector? Be my provider?"

Ah! It is in crossing that great divide where you place yourself totally in the hands of God that remains the secret that you will never know, until you cast away your fear. God demands from His children that they might know Him fully, and believe in His existence, but how can you do that unless you place your life within His hands? Are you willing to do that? That will be determined by the degree of fear and the lack of faith within you.

For this parent thing is two-way. It is two way inasmuch as God is saying, "Here I am, I am your protector and provider", and you are the other way, saying, "Should I really trust, really believe? What if He doesn't do these things?"

We cannot grow in faith until we place the faith that we have in a position where it will be tested. Then we will know the strength of the faith that we have. It is all very well and good saying, "I have faith in God". It means nothing. For you have heard the Lord Himself say, "If you had faith such as a mustard seed, you could say to the mountain, henceforth be cast into the sea", and it would obey you. Since you have not cast any mountains into the sea, you must consider how small a thing your faith is.

Faith cannot just be a feeling. It cannot be a void. It cannot be a substance, unless it is harnessed with intelligence and love. Then will it give to you that inner strength of knowing that nothing can harm you, and that all things you are capable of overcoming and doing. It will give to you the full measure of saying, "Yes Father, you are there, and I believe that you will do all things for me, and I will indeed trust my very life to you, for is it not you from whence it came? If it is love that you are teaching me, why then would you leave me to be destroyed?"

Isn't love the agreement and fulfilment of the law that says, 'We care for each other. We owe this duty'. As a father has a duty towards His children, so then has a sister towards her brother, and a brother towards his sister. The children to the mother and father, and the family to the uncles, aunts, and nephews, and to your neighbour, and to the unknown soul who is in difficulty, wherever he may be. YOU ARE YOUR BROTHERS', KEEPER.

This is what spiritual law means, but it must be firmly placed within your mind for you to be able to see it and understand it, and then to live by it. For unless you can live by it, then it means nothing. All your hopes and dreams, all your faith is without measure and is as worthless as dust, unless you live by it. It is putting it into your life, that makes the difference.

Only then will you be able to move things around you. To move the lives of others. To move your life into that inner circle where you may manipulate the power of spirit, the gifts of the spirit that God has given to all His children. But, you see, it can only be done by action. No-one can move a thing unless action is brought into being to move that thing. It has to be instilled within you, and be part of you. It must be you. You must see it, know it, and live it.

Our sister, earlier, was speaking about the various bodies that we have. The physical that you wear here and now, the soul body that we will pass into when we make that change called death, and then that soul body of the spirit which, in due course, will give way to the spirit. If you look at these things, all of them are governed by spiritual law. The physical body, the soul body, the spirit body. So it can truly be said that you are a spirit here and now. It can truly be said that you have free will to choose whichever way you wish to go, for the choice must always be there for you.

As that free will will serve no purpose unless it is motivated by knowledge, by wisdom, by understanding, it will not guide you to a favourable place where all your dreams will be fulfilled and your happiness complete, unless it is therefore, and must be, harnessed with intelligence. That intelligence is the same intelligence which must harness your faith. You must, with your free will, use that faith for the betterment of all.

You have used free will to bring you here. I have not done this. Nobody else has. You have come of your own free will. It is because you had a choice and see this as being the best choice. Because your intelligence, your commonsense, your understanding, have weighed up the differences that you could have gone, in a selfish, materialistic way, and perhaps destroyed all that you had.

You are beginning now to dress your personality with the cloth of spiritual worth. You are beginning to take upon yourselves, into the garment of humility, other yarns of goodness that will help you to open your spiritual eyes, and carry you forward if we wish to reach that point in time where we become the sons and daughters of God. When we reach that spiritual age of consent and we are the princes and princesses of the realm, then it is by our striving and by our motivation of knowing what is right and what is wrong.

You must not allow your fears to hold you back. Indecision is against your God, is against you. It prevents you from taking hold of that staff of faith and saying, "Father, here I am. Help me". You must rid yourself of that darkness, for it is a darkness. Fear comes and prevents you doing what you wish or what you want to do, and therefore it takes away from you your free will, your choice. It denies you this. That was never God's intention when He gave it to you.

If you are not going to have the strength to take full advantage of what He has given, then it were just as well He had never given it to you at all. Then what would you have been? You would have been subject to the will and the obsessions of all other things. Never a master of your own mind.

I cannot, in any way, make you different from what you are. I can tell you, and give you wise words which, you listening to may even agree that they are wise, and direct you into the paths of spirit. But you must act, no one else can do that for you. "I must act" you must say to this fear that rises up and prevents you from taking hold of the gifts that God has given you, "Be no more. Be silent. You are not my companion, and I shall not walk through life with you".

You shall say to caution, the spirit of caution, "Leave me and be no more, for I walk with God. I answer to His call, and I act according to the wisdom that He has instilled within me. I act to that spiritual awareness that comes to me and tells me what is right and what is wrong".

Only this way do you grow and begin to multiply in your spiritual knowledge. When all these things are embedded within you, and they are not just words that you have heard and they have been forgotten, but rather have come alive in you, have made themselves part of you, then will you begin to feel that force of life within yourself. That force of life that links you to the great God. Then will you understand more about His will, and how to perform that will, that it may be perfected in man, in this world.

Jesus, who spoke to you about the mustard seed, also said that those who came in later times will do all these things, and more. Remember this my children - all these things and more. Know the things that He spoke of were the miracles that He performed. You have the opportunity of fulfilling all that He said.

I doubt, until this present time, whether the things that are being told to you, have been said in exactly the same way. In exactly the same method, for the sole purpose of creating in you the complete awareness of who you are, and what you are to do with your life.

Remember how I have said to you in the past that it is essential for you to be free? At this moment of time, you are held bound by the things of earth, and by ignorance. You are wearing the chains of fear. You know not how to break free, how to use the great spiritual energies that are within you, but it will not always be so, for all things will pass. Change is inevitable. Just as yesterday may not seem much different from today, I tell you that in the years to come, you will look back and not be able to find this day. You have only got this day to work in. You have only got this day to change and reconstruct all the treasures of spirit anew, in you. You have only got this day to come to the true spiritual values. You cannot use yesterday, for it is gone. You cannot use tomorrow, for it is not yet come. So, always it is this day that you must use, and whatever you can accomplish in this day you must work towards.

You must grow in confidence of your own ability, to be able to create the things which are good. You must grow in awareness that the power of God is within your confidence, if you are working within His law. Nothing can tear down that law, or cause it to falter, even though you yourselves might fail in establishing that confidence within you, to that ultimate perfection where the will of God is within it. These must be your goals, and what you aim for today. You must always make the effort today, for while I say to you that you may have many other days to come, they are not today, and if you rely on 'tomorrow will do', you have wasted today. You can never, never recapture, take back or accomplish the things that could have been done today. That is gone for ever, and you will always be behind.

Your goal is your spiritual perfection. To perfect yourself, in love, in faith, in harmony with the universe, and with your God. In the fullness of spiritual knowledge and all that that means in power, to be in you, as you. It is only right that you should take up your rightful place, but you cannot do so unless you accomplish these things. Unless you become these things. This is what it means to come to the spiritual age of consent, and these are the things that you must learn as you learned in school as children the things of the earth - in order to reach the age of consent to how man knows the age of consent - so now you are aiming for spiritual consent. It is these things that you must establish in yourself, learn, and use each day to that end. As you are accomplishing your goal, think always within you that you are a child of God, and He has woken in you that special degree of love that makes you part of Him.

You have this unique position of knowing your heavenly Father, and being aware that you have but to call, and His will will be done with you, and whatever that will is, you will accept. Even if it isn't what you want, but you will accept.

The pains and the anguish of life are very often there to make you grow stronger and to give to you the power to fight. One day you will reach that point, one day you will be the sons and daughters of God. Not just a child, but the sons and daughters of God.

His law, His spiritual law will be working in, and through you, and in that same way, because it does, and because you understand you will be able to manipulate the very environment in which you live and create from it other things, just as Jesus did when He fed the five thousand, walked upon water, and forbad the storm, telling it to cease. All these things are the mark of the Son of God.

So, my children, you can see what lies before you. You can see the task that is there. Are you then going to become your own master, whereby you might take the clay of life, which is a virgin clay, and mould it into that life which you wish to have according to the design and will of God? That is your right. When He gave you free will, that became your right. Or shall you, like so many, allow that clay to be shaped according to events that happen to you caused by fear, doubts, and by the struggle to exist?

To him who will overcome, to him who will learn, to him who will grasp the full potential of faith, so then nothing can harm. Neither can fear be the thief that breaks in and steals your treasure, because you will be greater than them all.

When you are hungry, your Father will provide. When you are in danger, your Father will protect you. When you feel alone, He will comfort you with His love. If you do not like the life that you have, then change it. You have the will. Sit and think about what you will do and what you want to be and how you are to accomplish it. Enlist the aid of your God, that you may do just that.

Do not have fear and say, "Oh, if I do this, this might happen, and that might happen". You might just as well hide yourself in a deep dark cellar and stay there in case the light should shine upon you and your enemies see you.

In the spiritual realm to which you are one day to come, the fullness of your life will be realised. Little use is it that I should sit here with words, and try to paint the canvas of life, with that beautiful picture that is there waiting for you all. It is possible, for whatever I might say, whatever colour I might use to portray the picture, whatever wonderful brush-strokes I might use, it would just be but a very pale reflection of the actual truth.

It is like picking a daisy, and saying, "Look, a rose", or something like that. So, my children, you cannot bind yourself to the will of others, in order that they may do your will, or be held back. You can, by choice, bind your will to the will of the Lord, that you might travel with Him. How sweet a thing that would be, and how hard a thing that might be!

Forget not the pain that is involved in all these things. For I tell you, it is there. Sharp and clear. You will know from your testing time, exactly what I mean.

With these words I will bid you farewell my children, until the next time we meet.

Do not slumber and fall back into old ways, but awake and arise and be FILLED WITH THE MAGIC OF GOD.

A little food for thought: If God has a master plan for the salvation of mankind and we are His workers, what will happen if we are not in our places to lay the stone? The foundation will not be laid.

PARADISE AND QUESTIONS AND ANSWERS

Paradise cannot exist until you create it. It is a place waiting to be created, and of course if that is the case, paradise can be accomplished here on earth, although it would be extremely hard and difficult to do.

Q: Couldn't you build a wall around you, and make your own paradise?

A: The only way you could do that here, is to completely cut yourself off from the outside world and create a condition inside yourself that had within its folds all the sweetness of heaven. When I say this to you, what do you think are the main qualities required to build paradise? What do you think you would need?

You would need love, peace of mind, and contentment, You would also need the person you are in love with, to share your life.

They are a few of the requirements, and they will do for the time being, because out of them you may create other things also. For all these things are to become the very foundation and existence of paradise. That is what you must build upon to create that environment in which you would say you live in paradise.

You could not go to the extreme of saying that paradise is here in this world. It would have to be a separate condition which you have created out of the qualities of spirit, and built upon them the foundations and the environment which are totally different from the environment and the conditions of earth. In no way could you possibly include anything which is here, and say - that is paradise. All things here are subject to decay, subject to pollution, both in the poisonous things which man injects into his world, and also the poisons which come from his mind, of greed, and hatred, and selfishness. Things of that nature. None of those have the qualities which you require to build paradise. I am not saying that it could no be done, for it can be done. But it would be extremely difficult.

I want you to know that in the beginning before man fell from grace, he lived in paradise, and paradise was just a little way away from the world. When that condition of paradise was darkened and split up by another force entering into that environment that was not akin to its Maker, and thus destroyed it, man fell from grace to earth, and this was the place in that time where God created, firstly for the animal kingdom - which we came to share because we had fallen to the animal status, our own nature having become like animals.

We needed then to learn why it was that God said, "You may eat of every tree, but not the tree that groweth in the middle of the garden". We had directly broken His command. We were disobedient and had to be punished, not that God wants us to be obedient to every wish and whim that He has. There is so much more to it all than just that.

God knows that unless you respect and follow the order of life, and the environment in which you live, then you will be subject to great danger, for you will destroy the fabric of your world, and in turn destroy yourself. This indeed, is what is taking place now in your world, for are you not destroying the very environment that you so depend upon for life?

So then, when you say to me, "Is it possible to build a paradise here?" my reply to you is, that unless man DOES do this, then he has lost his battle, because the world will decay and crumble, and the essential life substance that he needs will no longer be there. Do not say to me that he has lost it, for that is a defeatist way of looking at things, and you are doing so without the knowledge of God. God has no intention that man should lose the battle. Indeed, He has a plan to bring man to salvation. And so shall He perform this act, and do just that.

I will not say every soul will be saved, for many have already perished, but I will say that all those who are of a like mind, and of a gentle nature, and are akin to that brother whom we call Lord of all, they will find their way home, and they will be given the bricks of paradise to build a world which is fit for the meek.

I am giving you all this, and I am very naughty, for it was not my intention to come and speak to you upon these matters. It was my intention to come and answer some of your questions. So I will leave this now, unless any of you take it up in a question.

Q: I was thinking along the lines of the Golden Age. Is that the same?

A: Yes. That is one and the same. If you recall, many years ago, I did say that one day I would come and speak to you upon the Golden Age, did I not? And can you see how far away we were from the idea and the ideologies and the perfection of the Golden Age at that time? It could not have been given then because its full text was not even in your minds. But now, over the years you have gradually been led this way, until already, the Golden Age is taking shape within you, and within your thoughts. This is the way that it happens. It is by the power of thought that you create. When I speak to you about the bricks of the Golden Age, I do not mean bricks of cement and sand, but the bricks of power provided by the qualities of your soul, in thought. That is what I mean. To bring it into being and breathe life into it. And all those who are enclosed within it, live in the Golden Age.

Of course the Golden Age is one which is totally free from the discomforts that you wear upon your mind, your heart, and your body, here and now. They have been and can be dissolved. It is not necessary. In the very, very first instance, it was never God's intention that man should suffer in this way. It was his choice, you see. Mans' choice, never God's.

As soon as man is ready to accept that very first thought as a seed to the great life that can be his, then God is willing and waiting to push him in that direction. Any more questions?

Q: You said in one of your previous talks that mans' thinking was all wrong, and you said it was the power of thought generated with the power of salvation. What did you mean by this? Generated by the power of Salvation?

A: I do not know the full text of what you are referring to, but if I might say these things for you to understand - It is the power of thought that is creative. It creates. And you may use that form of creation in what ever way you choose. For good, or for bad.

If you choose for the bad, then you can plainly see the result already in your world, can you not? If you choose for the good, then you are using your thoughts for the creation of salvation. Do you see that? And it is up to those with the power of God, to work for the salvation of all men. Meaning, to free them from the ignorance and darkness in which they live. The world they have created. Do you see that? That they may turn their thoughts from the dark side of their natures, to the light side, and create for the good of all mankind.

Wouldn't it be a wonderful thing, if tomorrow morning the world woke up, and when they did so, they were alive to the full reality of God and the full potential that lies within them in the gifts of the spirit, and the power of their thinking to make manifest a world which meant freedom for all God's children. Then no more would they want, no more would they be diseased, no more would there be anguish, fear or suffering of any description. Then the world might prosper, and grow in the beauty that God first set it down in. When nature reigned supreme, with all her children arrayed in the earth each spring and summer - the flowers, the grass, the tall trees. All of this is part of your true nature. It is the true nature of God.

Q: It is part of selflessness, then?

A: Yes. Totally, completely. To free yourself of every dirty morsel of thought that impairs and creates that condition that brings unhappiness. Do you understand?

Q: Can I ask what might appear to be a disrespectful question?

A: Ask what you will.

Q: Since God created all things, including mankind, why was it necessary for Him to create us with a dark side to our nature as well as a good side? Could it not be said that because He created us in this way, that He also created evil?

A: I understand your question, and I understand what is in your mind, but of course you know, unless you have a choice, there is no progression, because if you take the road, the only road that leads to God, and there is no other, then all will lead to God. You will have done so without having been either been tried, or tested.

Of course it has always been God's purpose, since man fell from grace, that he should know why he had come to earth and fought the battle of life. For if he chose to become as Gods, then he must have the understanding of Gods. He must be able to use his power as Gods, and the only way he can do that, is to discover for himself what is right, and what is wrong. discover for himself what is best for him. When he discovers that, then he will discover that it cannot be for him alone, but must be for all mankind. And thus he begins to work to that end. Whether it be in the same way as I or my son (Douglas Arnold) who I use, or you, when you too take up the challenge, and bear the cross before you. Or whether it is just simply in his own way, with his friends, to state his opinion and his belief. The change from the harshness of that character and nature that belongs to the physical body, to that soft and gentle nature that belongs to the God-man that he is striving to become.

Yes indeed you may say, "Did God create evil?". No, He did not. Because the two comparisons have always been there. Just as two and two make four, and did not need anyone to create that, for it existed, then do you have light and dark, good and evil, love and hate. because YOU exist. They exist because, out of them both, you must choose. The evil will teach you about the good, and the good will teach you about the evil. Now that may sound very strange, but it is quite true. Each of them teaches you about the other. They did not need to be created, they are. They just simply are.

So you continue through your life, and through the exchanges of your experiences, you come to the better way. You come to the God mans' way. As it is written, 'Know ye not you are all Gods?' So must you become. Because of that, you must learn the way of the light, the way of truth, the way of love, for the darkness will show you. It will show you what is there in the paths of evil. If it is that your nature says, that is suffering, and I seek for peace, then it will turn you to the light. For only in the light will you find that joy and happiness that you seek for. But even though you have come to know what it is that you are seeking for, it will not shield you against the darkness, but rather bring that force of power viciously against what you are striving to achieve. For it is like, if you will, the fires of hell, burning within you, and burning you to pure gold.

Out of that will come this total dislike and hatred for all that which is of a destructive nature. They are two powers that are there, and you may use them. You may give them life, either one of them. You will not find any of the prophets or holy man, in times past, that had an easy life. They did not. Their lives were constantly being challenged, because it was the way they wished to live their lives. And the things they believed in were also constantly being challenged, but it was the spirit within, and fight within, and the strength within to do what is good, that overcame the powers of darkness, that threatened to take away their very existence. It cannot do that. To him who overcomes, all things are possible. And that is where you stay.

It is, I know, in your world, a typical view that God created everything. He did not. You will discover that quite a lot of other things are there, because that is the way of things. They did not need anyone to create them, they are there. If I could find a better way of using your words to put it more clearly, I would, but I cannot. It defies the use of words to describe exactly what I mean. All I can say to you, is that they are there because they are there. I can give you no real answer other than that. Both of them in their turn, will teach you about the other. Out of that you will choose, and you will surely choose the light. But, of course, there are always some who will never choose the light, because they have gone too deeply into the darkness. As it is written, 'As ugly as sin', then you see, that is what they become. When that happens, then there is no longer the commonsense for them to see what is happening. They are governed completely by the forces of darkness, in order for it to control their lives. They have become absorbed in it all.

You have the land, you have the sea. It is like that. One is dry, and one is wet. You can live in the sea or you can live on dry land, Invariably the sea will take your life, because it is not conducive to the environment of your body. If you live on the land through your own choice you can also lose your life if you seek to do things which are contrary the laws of the land, and I think that I have already stated that today, that is what man is doing. Do you understand me?

Time has gone swiftly. I had hoped to answer more questions. The length of each answer depends upon the type of question, and if a full answer is to be given, then it will take time. We will have others - other meetings such as this, and we will perhaps have two or three, one after the other, in order to give everyone the chance to think of and ask that question upon which they do not readily understand. I will bid you good day, one and all. God be with you.

THE COIN OF LOVE

In the morning when the sun has risen, you look upon a new day. The emphasis is on the 'new'. It is not meant to be linked with yesterday, neither is it meant to be carried forward to the following day. It is a new day which your God has given to you. A new opportunity to make good the mistakes of yesterday. A new day to create for yourself something of spiritual value.

Now Jesus said to "Keep your treasure where neither moth nor rust nor thief can enter in and steal it away". Quite obviously He was not speaking about your earthly treasure, He was speaking about your spiritual treasure. Indeed, you have a way of living here that is designed by man, and because of that you do need to obey the laws of man. You need the coin of the realm in order to purchase your needs.

There IS a coin of the realm in that far country that you have come from, that spiritual land, to which you all really belong, that kingdom which, in the Lord's prayer, you ask to come. It is just as spendable as that coin which you know here. For the coin of the realm in God's kingdom, is love. You earn that coin, just as you earn the coin that you have here.

You earn it by your good deeds. You earn it by compassion, by your sincerity, by your forgiveness, by your friendship, by your kindliness, and by your willingness to give to those less fortunate than yourself. There is no paymaster. No one comes on a set day and says, "Here are your wages for the week", for the coin does not work in the same way that yours does on earth. It is the love you receive from others. The love that they give you, and the love that you give in return that is your treasure in heaven. Where neither moth nor rust nor thief can enter in, and steal it.

This is why you need that compassion, forgiveness, kindliness and friendliness, because that is the labour of love, and the labour is what I meant when I said you need to earn that coin. That is the way it IS earned, because you generate within, all the warmth that brings alive that love from others.

You do not have to wait to make the change called death before you can begin to earn the coin of love. You can begin now, by your dealings with others.

I want you to see that love therefore, is even more important than the milk that is given to a young babe, and well you know that without that milk the young child cannot be sustained, and its life would flicker away. I want you to see that love, has that same power to sustain YOUR life, and create conditions in which heaven itself is made. It is the very substance, the very materials that you require, in order to create that heaven.

It is the atmosphere in which we in the spirit world live. It is as important to us, as the air itself is to you. It is our environment. An environment in which each one of you must come and live, sooner or later. No one can escape it, for all who live on the earth must make the change called death and live in that new environment.

To many, in the beginning, it is not an easy thing, because their whole world has been turned upside down, Especially for those who have held positions of power in your world, and have been used to having others fetch and carry for them, for they will learn that it is now THEIR turn to do the fetching and carrying.

For somebody like this, life can be difficult. Their fame that followed them on earth no longer follows them there. Their domineering features which they exercised over lesser men, no longer work for them over there.

Where they could put fear into the hearts of the lesser man by threatening him with the law, and by all kinds of other things which man is subject to on earth, like losing his work, his home, or not having enough to feed his family with, does not apply there. He will find that he is bankrupt. All the wealth he had is gone, and because he never worked to put any SPIRITUAL currency into his bank, he will have few who will love him, and love is the power that brings happiness, brings him a fullness of life, but it will no longer be there, because all those who worked under him, were afraid of him. He also exercised the authority that his wealth gave him, and as the baby cannot live without milk, so neither can he live in the kingdom of heaven without love. Difficulties will be strewn across his path.

The greatest difficulty that will be there, will be his inability to forgive himself. When he comes to the fires of remorse that Jesus spoke of, he will come to see that all his actions here on earth have brought him only grief and sadness. He will have been the eye witness, the jury, and the judge, of all those things that he committed. So you can see how difficult it would be for him. Much harder for him to progress in that new state of being than here, for he will have found himself in the desert of life, totally void of the things of life, for it will be what he has created while here on earth.

I give you this example because I want you to see the importance of striving during your life on earth, to acquire that coin of love, and to realise that you cannot expect to receive, unless you first give. Yes, as you give, then so you shall receive. You have heard this said many times I am sure. You can realise, listening to that story, just what it means: AS YOU GIVE, SO WILL YOU RECEIVE.

To him who has given love, love shall he receive. That will be his coin to send in the life to come. That will be the way in which he will begin to evolve. Not so here.

So my children, I want you to consider LOVE. Consider it, because in all the experiences of your life, they are so designed to bring you to the knowledge of love. You have been given that free will in which to answer that problem which is set before you. You will come to see and realise that all things are very cold, empty and meaningless, unless you have that quality of love.

It was not the man's wealth, importance or position that brought him to poverty on the other side of life. It was his neglect of love. It matters not what position you hold, or how powerful a position you have been given in life, so long as you remember that love is the key that opens your Father's door.

Love is the coin that will purchase for you that fuller life, when this one is finished. You CAN journey on in that realm in complete happiness and in a state of joy and contentment that you would not have believed possible.

Your loving Father has done all this with the fulfilment of your spiritual coming of age in mind. There are now many things in your world that corrupt and destroy the opportunity for the fulfilment of mans' free will and spiritual evolvement. Because of this, God must intervene and prevent it from continuing on. Unless He does, then His gift that He has given you, will come to nought and cause you great suffering.

He will not allow His children to have His purpose within them, defeated by the designs of greedy men. Man has already taken the step that ensures that that intervention must come, for unless it comes, no flesh can remain on earth. All will perish.

GOD HAS NO INTENTION OF ALLOWING THAT TO HAPPEN.

The things that are set before you along the road of life, are there inasmuch as they bring to you a great deal of fear about the sufferings which happen. They also bring to you the assurance, that all is going to be well. Even though you must wait and see what develops, and how it evolves. But IT WILL HAPPEN. For the LAW of God WILL BE DONE. The WILL of God WILL BE DONE.

Our Father who art in heaven, hallowed be Thy name. Thy kingdom come, Thy will be done, on earth, as it is in heaven. IT CANNOT BE ANY OTHER WAY.

I cannot stay long today, and I must leave you there. I would like to think that we do not finish there, but you will talk about what has been said, not just today but on other occasions, and perhaps work out solutions for yourself.

Good afternoon one and all, and God bless you.

AGGRESSION

A member of Mr. Arnold's group having read from Corinthians 1, Chapter 12, Hafed begins to speak...

The mood has been set for us by the reading itself, and if I am able, I would like to show you the reasons why love must be the most potent power within you, and within the motivation of your soul, to do God's work.

Firstly, I do not believe that you have need for me to tell you that God is love, therefore, He is the figurehead, the fountain of life, the fountain of joy, the fountain of happiness. But perhaps what is even more important, He is the holiness within that love, for His love is not the same that a man has for a woman or vice versa, or for their children. His love is a holy love, and is far deeper and far more enriched with that sincerity that must fill your breast when you serve God. Love is honest, and honesty was the first quest that I gave you. The first step towards God.

Love is pure, and therefore cannot in any way be deceitful. Can in no way be one which is untrue. There are many aspects to love which is God's love, for when it comes to you it will refine you of all the impurities that life has there for you now. It will give you not only the qualities of spiritual love and holiness, but give to you a light of truth.

Love has that ability, to take the life of a man and change it completely, and fill it with an awareness of where he is going wrong, and make him feel all that which he should be doing, and is not.

So far, what I have said to you has been in word form. It is like a pointing finger, that directs your spiritual mind into that path that we would see you pursue. In no way has it been able to inject in you any of its true emotions and feelings.

When you speak one to the other, it is in word form, it is in sound that reaches your ears. If it has not that quality of love within it, then it is empty and meaningless, and has not the ability to touch the soul of another and stir within it that true love that you feel for each other.

You can only inject that kind of emotion and power into your words when you have that true spiritual love within you, and that my children, will make positive contact with the mind and soul of that wretched soul that you are trying to uplift and bring to the light. To make him aware of the greatness that God is.

When you come to the full realisation of this wondrous love, then your life will change. It will change in a way of being totally different from the one that you have made for yourself now.

It has the ability to make you aware that no harm can come to you and that the true purpose of life is not found in the fulfilment of earthly things, but in the fulfilment of your spiritual quest. The quest of the soul. That can only be when you have the full measure of God's love, for it is when the holy spirit is motivating your every action and bringing you to that point where you no longer reside in a physical body, although you do, but more within the soul body, which is bound up in the spiritual mind.

Yes, you are here in a physical state, that is true, but not to carry out the physical law, or to be ruled or governed by the temptations that that physical law presents to you, that you might fall.

I have often told you that you will be tempted, by many different things in life. Also, you will fall, because you are not yet the **full** measure of those temptations which come. This is due to the fact that you are evolving, from the child of God to the sons and daughters of God. In that unfoldment, both in the spiritual and mindful way, so come the temptations from the physical body.

It is like being reborn, but this time as a child of light that you have heard is to come in this era of time. But when we speak to you of a child, we do not mean the new babies being born, but the child of God, the spiritual child that you are struggling to become - to give birth to, and all the experiences, all the temptations you are being presented with, are to enlighten your awareness and your spiritual understanding.

Now love is the ultimate goal that you must reach. Do not just listen to my words, although I know that those words cannot possibly reach you in the same way that I would like them to, but they will reach you according to your spiritual light within, your awareness within. What you are prepared to give, not only to your God, but to others.

Love is the complete sacrifice, and this is the ultimate joy that you are to reach. When you consider love, and say it is the ultimate sacrifice, you must realise those words, and the fulfilment of them No man has greater love than this, than he should lay down his life for his friend. Jesus did this for us. He laid down His life, that the greater light of truth might shine down through the ages of man, and bring that spiritual birth of the child of light.

So we are, therefore, looking at something that perhaps you are not wholely prepared to do. What ARE you prepared to do for your neighbour and your friend who sits by your side? Do you really love them? Or is there a barrier that stands between you? Is there a coldness that is still there? For if there is, all that you do is meaningless, and can in no way accomplish anything. You may have proven that that person has been hurtful to you, and caused this themselves, but that still does not in any way, provide you with the right to retaliate.

That is something that cannot be part of God's law. It does not in any way fulfill the forgiveness side of the nature that must be inherent in the children of God. You have the right to forgive, my children, but you do not have the right to judge. That is what love does. It weaves those things together for you, and makes it complete. The forgiveness complete.

It makes you able to touch the souls of others with words that go deep. It does this, not by them knowing the meaning of the words for we all know the meaning of the words, but that is not sufficient. You have to FEEL the power that is there. You have to KNOW what it really is.

This is the state of spirituality that you are striving to achieve, and by our coming to you like this in this sweet way each week, it is our hope that we can gradually reveal to you exactly what you must be doing to accomplish that. That feeling of love. Not the words, not the meaning, but the FEELING of love. That it is embodied within you and changes your life, for you then are able to see exactly where you are going.

It will drive out all your fears, your petty jealousies and hatreds. All that which you call boredom, because it is the very energy of life that gives complete joy and contentment.

It is the light that shines within truth - the light of Christ, and will not permit darkness to enter. Fear cannot dwell there, for you already know the supreme power of all-being, to be your God, your Father, your Creator, and therefore there can be no one that you fear.

That, my children, is where we are trying to lead you, step by step. Of course it is necessary for us to go over and over the same ground, time after time. Perhaps in different ways, with different ideas being at the centre, but always pointing you in the same direction, so that eventually it may all click into place and you might say, "Ah yes, of course! I know now! I KNOW now!" And that is when the child is born. The child of light. The child of love.

My children, we must drive out from within you all that which is called aggression. For all the people of the world have aggression. It is found in your work-a-day life with your colleagues, it is found in the home between members of the family, it is found between your friends and neighbours. It is found between governments of different nations, and it is found in the sports that you like to watch. It is a poison which is destroying all that which is to bring you to salvation.

It is slowly destroying the earth on which you live. It is slowly numbing your minds to love, and preventing that feeling from existing between man and woman, and sons and daughters. Aggression. We must give consideration to this, for it is not in any way part of the law of God, and never ever can be.

You have been given free will, and it can be broken down into two parts. One is freedom, which free will means. Freedom is willpower. Willpower by which you accomplish you aims in life. But if it is motivated by aggression, then it is a destroyer of your life and a destroyer of your freedom, and is in no way a creative energy, which so often I have spoken to you as being a soul deliverer from all your angers, all your hatreds, and your wants and fears, all your anxieties.

You sit in the quiet and you wonder about your life and about what you are trying to accomplish, but always there is that aggression still with you. It is a part of your nature that you have built up over the course of time, here on earth. You have copied this from others, you think to yourselves that if you want to get on in life, you have got to have this aggression to win, for to win is the only thing. But I say you, if to win by means of aggression is the only way, then better for you that you never win at all.

This is the image that has been created by man and his aggression - the will to win, but in order for us to win with aggression, he forgets freedom. He forgets that somewhere he is going to take away freedom from others.

That is his first mistake, for he cripples the spiritual progression of another. The will to win through aggression can achieve only one thing - YOUR DESTRUCTION. It cannot create for you a spiritual balance of power by which you will succeed. For when you say 'the will to win', you are speaking about yourself, and you are but one, an individual.

The will to win for all, FOR ALL THROUGH LOVE is something far greater. But it is a different image than the one which hangs in the prize place of mans' mind, the will to succeed through aggression. The will to win through love, means to win for all. Means to bring happiness and joy to all men, that all may be equal, that all may stand in the light of God's sun, that all might be free from fear and hunger, want, and disease.

These truly are the goals that man should be setting for himself, and if he did so, then you can see the great advancement that the world would make. He would free himself from the fears of war, famine, and disease, Especially those diseases which come from mans' own lust, for he creates the imperfect seed.

The imperfect seed that fulfills the saying which says, 'The sins of the fathers shall visit the children', and thus it is already happening. You see this, and it is a great sin, a great cross to bear, because it is imperfect seed created out of imperfection. Created out of those energies that destroy, and not create. The energies of lust and greed. The energies of hatred and violence. The energies of aggression are all there, creating that seed of imperfection, designed in the shape of sin, that tortures and totally annihilates mankind.

I do hope my children, that I am not worrying you by what I am saying, or causing you to be fearful, but I cannot bring the truth to you unless I tell you and show you the exact picture of what is taking shape here and now, so that you may guard yourselves against that way of life.

To seek for the treasures of heaven which as we know are bound up in love, in God, and in all of us if we are prepared to surrender our will to His, and to sacrifice our lives for the lives of lesser men of lesser understanding.

So my children, you might see that the garb of aggression is worn by the deceiver, and cannot and will not ever enter into the realms of light, but can only find its place according to its own spiritual value and its own agony and pain.

That is why we must take seriously, aggression. For remember aggression takes its shape and its form in many different ways - in violence, cheating, and in wrong thinking, aggression is there. Deceit also is born from the womb of aggression.

You must examine your lives, your thoughts, and your relationships with each other, as well as your friends, neighbours, and those with whom you work, in order to put yourselves in the right frame of mind to address them and to love them. For if God is able to love you who are imperfect, and loves all others who are sinful to say the least, then should we not be able to love each other? Above all, to love God.

Do not forget to tell God that you love Him. He likes to be told. For in that word 'love' there is a vibration of love which can be returned to you one hundred fold. So, when you say, "Father, I love you", you will feel that uplift of love come into your being, and you will know that He has answered you by saying, "I love you too, my child". Soft and gentle is His way. That too, is how you must be.

I will leave these thoughts with you to dwell on and digest, that you might become sober minded and find the delight of knowing God that much close than you have ever known Him before.

At some later stage we will speak again about aggression, how it defaces the beauty that is to be found in some of the skills in your sport. By showing you that it defaces the souls of men, in their actions in life.

I will ask you first if you have any questions that you would like to ask, before I depart?

Q: How do you treat someone who harms you when you have constant contact with them? Obviously you don't return the harm, but do you ignore them, or do you cut yourself off from them?

A: Ignore is a word I do not like for it is a base word, which means that it is your revenge. We will not hide our faces from the truth, but we will face the reality of God's teaching. The way, is to love them.

Q: Just pretend that nothings happened?

A: No, pretence is not the word. Pretence again, is part of deceit, and cannot in any way have part in solving your problem. You love them, and you SHOW them that you love them. You forgive them each time that their actions or their tongue digs a little deeper into you.

Q: I am not saying that I disagree with you, but in that way, you are almost pretending to them that you haven't even noticed what they have done. Is that what you mean?

A: It is not a pretence. It is simply that you are spiritually aware of their inability to love you back, but because they have that inability, you do not hurt them in return, you love them, for they are incapable of loving to that degree. By showing them, by demonstration, you will then win. because you will take the sword from their hand. At the same time it is also advisable to examine yourself too, in the light of what they are saying, to see if perhaps there is any truth there.

Q: It isn't something someone has said, it is what they have done.

A: I see. But that is what you must do. You must forgive them, and you must love them back. I would not say that if someone was causing you physical harm you should allow it to continue. The law of the land does not permit such a thing, and neither does the law of God. That deems punishment of some description, whether it is a term of imprisonment or a fine or whatever. There has to be a form of punishment.

Even so, it does not mean to say that you must hold your forgiveness back from them. That forgiveness is yours to give, and is rightfully so. To love is the only way you can forgive, for that is the only complete way. To say that I will not have anything to do with them is one way, for you do not have to go near a violent person when you know his intention is to harm you. But rather, if you hold your hurt and without your forgiveness and love, remember that this is causing greater harm than the punishment of the physical body, and so is destroying your spiritual light. You cannot progress in heaven unless you forgive. That is a necessity. As you forgive others, so God will forgive you. It is in your prayer, (the Lord's prayer), take full advantage of it.

Q: I do know that we must forgive, its just how to treat them on earth.

A: With love. With love and forgiveness. It does not mean that you must go out of your way to be a friend to them, although it would be nice if that could happen. That could only happen if they would be a friend to you. It is perhaps better to remain aloof, still forgive them and love them, but have no further dealings with them. Do you understand?

Now it is time for me to depart and so I will bid you good afternoon. God bless you all.

THE CLEANSING POWER OF COMPASSION

The tape was blank between 0-70. The talk thus far consisted in content of an explanation of how and why it is that we, and others like us, view pain and suffering in our brothers and sisters on earth, with such anguish. The tapes continues ....

....the whole terrible truth is being reflected and seen. It is not a woven tapestry that is before you, and thus gives you a spiritual picture that you can see, or a piece of jigsaw that has fallen into place and made the picture come to life. It is none of these things, but it is that indwelling knowing - that spiritual awareness that is growing in you, and awakening you to the Christ spirit that is there. That spirit that cries to you 'Abba Father', for you are being born, as it were, the sons and daughters of God. Your time for the coming of age is approaching, and that is why you see it, that is why you feel it so deep within you.

Alas, while you see and feel all this, and know it within you, there is something lacking. Something that you do not know, and I for my part find it terribly difficult to put into words, and that is the coming alive of the events that you see.

How they are conjured, woven, into this nightmarish dream? How was it all brought together? What happened?

To discover this, you must have a very good basic understanding of spiritual law at work within you, and material law that is at work within the world. The meeting place you see, for the two, for there has got to be that - a meeting place for the two. The spiritual law, must meet, for one is to feed the other if there is to be harmony and unity between the two.

How can I put into words that they become substance in your mind, things which are of spiritual origin, and have sounds to them that you have never heard before? How can I enrich your soul so that it may see and feel that difference that lies between them?

When your mind is alive with spiritual truth there is a force-field, a spiritual force-field, which is enclosing your mind, your soul, your body. It is encircled with that potent power of life, and it is the very emblem where the two meet, the carnal and the spiritual. For the energy and the light that are there in that force field, are revealing to you life in a much fuller potential than anything else. It was always meant by the Father that this should be so, and that you, His children, should be, as it were, protected.

It is that very spot where the smallest atom of materialism is given life, and takes on life through the spiritual power that is there. I wonder if you can see that picture that I want you to see? That very place where the two meet. Remembering that the whole of your body is made up of atoms and electrons, and various other chemicals that are born out of them, given life by an energy that is not known to mankind, because it is of a. God power.

It is not electricity, for that came later. It is a power that is of life itself, and the two are fused together. That makes up your body, for that holy power, that force of life, is a cleansing power. All material substance will decay and die, and indeed would not take on life if it was not for the meeting point between the spiritual power of life, and materialism. It is like, almost to be seen as, a virus, for it is that tiny. A place where they congeal and bring forth life in the material body.

All this first takes place through your mind, and thus you will begin to see and understand, why the importance of compassion. Why the importance of love and forgiveness, For the breakdown of those harmonious patterns create within you a fall in compassion, and give way to that greater degree of mans' determination to hold a position of power.

It is incompatible with God's law, that you maintain one level of spiritual awareness. It is that spiritual awareness then, that holds you above the falling down, and the taking on of hatred, greed and mans' own destructive thoughts that burn him away, and send into the world such diseases that you now have with you. For when you are seeing what you ARE seeing in the world, remember that is only the outward expression, it is NOT the actual cause. The law of causes and effect. The cause is this, the effect is that.

If then, by keeping your soul filled with that spiritual light, and your mind burning with that light of compassion you allow God's power to come into your world, God's power is a cleansing agent, that cleans and purifies and multiplies light.

If you allow that light to go out, and hold the darker side of your nature, so that the reverse thing happens, then the thoughts that go out are of a destructive element that tears down, and breeds disease into the world.

You may ask how this happens, and what we are discussing is the very fringe of that indestructible section of creation. We are on the very fringe, and I know that it is terribly difficult for you to understand what I mean, what I am saying, but you must have a beginning, you must start somewhere, and this is the level that I have chosen for you to start at, so that you may gradually come to understand and see that the energy forces that you are releasing into your life, and into the world, are deemed by your spirituality, by your compassion. Those on your side of life can see that, for your light is one which shines out like a beacon in the darkness.

Those who are filled with mans' inhumanity to man are of a different light. Like a fiery light. As if their soul was burning up. That is what they radiate. They destroy.

Now this is the point where we are in time. I want you to see how all of this links together under one law - the spiritual law, that even governs the material law. To turn away from that is to destroy even the fabric of materialism. To destroy it. For materialism is clean so long as it is being charged with the energies of God. When it is no longer so, then it is breaking down all the time that fabric.

You have an environment in which you live, but that environment is only being kept by the fabric of materialism that begins to form at the fringe. Spiritual life meets material life, and it is that energy that is being injected into those atoms that is maintaining your own environment and which keeps you alive.

When that begins to break down, so then does the law and power that governs Mother Nature. She is linked together, and her link cannot and MUST never be broken, for this would mean the end of mankind.

The force and power that is in Mother Nature, which is life-giving because it is bound up in the energies of water, the energies of fire, the energies of Mother Nature, that provides for the flowers, the food, and the raw materials that support man - when these things begin to break down and become polluted as they are, then they begin to die. Do you see what I mean?

Because they begin to die, they decompose and become the diseases that come into your world and attack your bodies in the form of germs and viruses which are totally unknown to your doctors and scientists, and will not be overcome.

If that deterioration is allowed to continue, then only madness can come to man, because he is going away from the peace of mind and commonsense that holds his sanity. When he goes down below that, then is madness that he comes to and the world at large will be no more.

Now this is the problem that you have in your world, and you can see now how vital it is for man to inject compassion into his life.

At this point I want to stop. I do not want to feed you too much that perhaps you are not really understanding. I want to ask you, that if you don't understand fully what I have told you, then tell me what is, and I will do my best to try and put it in a way that you CAN understand. Any Questions?

Q: What did you mean by being 'On the fringe of creation'?

A: You must realise that creation has a point, a place where it starts. An injection of energy and life that gives Mother Nature the power to exist. Do you understand what I mean? Therefore there is a place, a beginning, whereby that power of life is fused with the atoms of materialism, The more solid substance, if you like, that is what builds up and creates the world at large and sustains it. That is the important thing, it sustains it. It recharges the energies of growth and keeps alive all the material factors that produce food and energy for mankind to live.

So that is the point where it all begins. It wasn't simply something that happened, and there behold - a solid world appears. It had to have a time of creation, a point of creation. That was the point, where materialism took on the energies of life.

Q: Does that mean that this is the beginning of creation - Where it begins?

A: That is right.

Q:Here, on earth?

A: It begins; let me see if I can clarify your mind. The kind of creation that I speak of, is not of the soul. So do not make the mistake of thinking that that was where you were created as a living soul. It is the point where all the other things were created and from the source of that power came all things. Like the earth that you stand on, the trees, the rivers, the wind, the sun, your physical body, and animal kingdom, and the insect kingdom. All these things were formed out of that creation.

I suppose scientists will say that it was formed out of gases which cooled down, and so forth and so forth. But there is another part which comes BEFORE that. It comes from that meeting place of the spiritual power and the atoms of materialism. They all congealed together in order to build and create the world in which you live. The very gases of which man speaks were formed because of that joining together. Do you understand me?

Q: It seemed to me that while you were talking, I was having a picture drawn in my mind of two separate things or substances with a dividing line between them - imperceptible, but a definite dividing line between them. But that from one was filtering down all the way through it, something into the other one that the other one required to keep it in existence.

A: That is so.

Q: But all of a sudden, that begins to slow down, and it was because of the change in the second substance, that whatever it was that was filtering down, could not get through, and was gradually being blocked off. Is that right?

A: That is right. That is absolutely right. If, you see, mans' mind, and the thoughts of man, as well you understand it to be, are of a creative element, then you must see that it is very necessary for those thoughts of men to be filled with the right source of love and compassion in order for that law - that spiritual power, to stay in existence.

When Mans' thoughts begin to fall, and bring it down by his own actions, and his own thoughts of creation, then he is warring against the law of God, and the true creative element that, in itself, will cause the destruction of nature and ultimately the world. Now man can witness this happening in the forms of acid rain, chemicals pouring into the rivers, and the destruction of the rain forests. It can also be seen in various other aspects like oil spillage at sea, the ozone layer and widespread use of pesticides which not only kill off the birds and wildlife, but bring much illness and disease to humans. Indeed man is causing untold damage by his pollution of the land, sea, and air.

What man fails to appreciate, is that he is witnessing the law of CAUSE and EFFECT in operation. He sees only the effect, without realising that the cause lays within HIMSELF. It is only because he has fallen from grace and taken hold of this mans' inhumanity to man, that he is creating the very substance which is poisoning all these things.

It is born out of his greed and ignorance, whereas if he truly stayed in the life of God's peace and love, that would not and could not happen, because he would see that that is wrong. That all forms of poison are wrong. Mother Nature is perfectly capable of controlling her own law in her own way. She can sustain the earth and all things in it, including the environment.

When the environment is beginning to suffer, then it is breaking down Mother Nature's chain that is forged together. If and when one of those links break, then it is the collapse of life as you know it or understand.

That is what we on the other side are fighting against. This is why you have got this so-called 'Spiritualism' in your world. That is mans' name, mans' idea, it is not ours.

Many of my brothers who come from the realms of light, come with that weapon of power in the words that we convey to you - of truth, that will combat the very ignorance of man, and destroy mans' inhumanity to man, so that the flower of compassion may again blossom forth and fill his mind with that Christ spirit which is life eternal, and joy eternal, and happiness eternal. So, all over your globe at this time as I speak, there are little groups like yourselves. You are comrades in arms, for you are all learning about the same things, and you are all fighting the same cause. Your destiny and destination is the same.

In the words that we give, in the truth that we give, it will open out your heart and your mind and give to you the zeal to fight. The realisation, that you have nothing, unless you do. That you must be by your Lord's side and create with Him, that new world that is prophesied.

This is what your whole life is about, and always has been. Even before you were born, you were so charged with this - sent as it were, to link together and form the basis and the nucleus of that power that is unstoppable, because it has the creative energies of God. No one no man, no power, can destroy it, only through negative thinking, by becoming weak when you are under attack from the powers of darkness, as surely you will be, because you hold the truth. They will try in every way to turn your thoughts, to make you question your God.

When your life seems to go wrong, that will give them the edge to use against you, and say, "Where is your God now?" And you will think that YOU are saying it' You will think that they are YOUR thoughts! But they are not, and it begins to make your faith wane, and separates you from your God.

But, little ones, remember this! Never can you do anything wrong, so bad, that your Heavenly Father has not already given you His forgiveness. For He is understanding. He understands.

Because I give you truth of this calibre, and I have said it before, and I will say it again, I do you no favours. For now you are responsible for the truth that I have given to you, and because you are responsible, you have a responsibility to those others who are lesser than you in their understanding of God, but equal to you in the fact that they belong to God's family. You are trying desperately to set them free, even those with most evil minds, because they are held captive by ignorance and darkness. So I do you no favours.

You are now free of the law that man has made. You are bound by that spiritual law that God has made. To Him and only Him, to no judge of this world are you answerable. You are set free, with that power of salvation in your words, to meet and speak and reveal the mysteries of God.

Do not fear, for you do not travel alone. There are those comrades in arms who are also sojourning with you from the other side of life. Those teachers, friends, and helpers. They are legions strong.

Think not to yourself that though God has not been able to lift a small trouble from you, that He is not able to do those things which are far greater. I tell you, that in the twinkling of an eye, you shall be changed, and the will of God cannot be opposed. Neither can the power of God be defeated.

Very often man forgets just how great God is. He forgets that He is capable of all things. That in your life, yes, in your life, you will be reminded of these things, by Him who is your Father, for surely those days will come when you will see His power at work, and those miracles done before you.

So, let peace reign amongst you. For you surely can see how important that is. For if you do not have that love, one towards the other, how can you have love for those you do not know? Or who are of a different culture, a different colour, believe in different things to you? But you must, you see. You must.

So let peace be that power that binds you together. Let it be so with love. For well now you understand what can come.What destructive nature and thoughts that are less than these can bring.

Before I go, is there one more question?

Q: Yes. Will our planet get worse? I mean, its full of diseases now which are incurable. Will we have much more?

A: It is a thing I do not want to touch upon too deeply, but of course, there are events which are to come, which are worse than that you have experienced in the past. Of course, all these things must be so, for the dawning of that new day and that new world. More than this I will not say, except to say that these things are close at hand, and on the wings of tomorrow you will see them.

Q: Not very long ago, you said that man had taken the final step that would lead to his destruction. Is it a combination of all these things you have mentioned, or is it something specific like radiation?

A: It is all part of the same picture. For all of that comes from mans' desire to control power. Greed is the downfall of this planet. Greed most surely, because that is the root of everything, isn't it? Greed, fear, lust, and evil that stems from those who have already lost their mind to madness. Pray then, that a madman does not come to power, and oppose what good there is in the world. But, like I said, the day will then dawn when a great brightness comes, and the Lord Himself with return.**

There are other great things that I must speak to you of, that you have not heard before, and when the time is right, I shall reveal them, but for a little while longer we will concentrate more on what I have already given to you, and see how this has been established in your minds - what kind of a foundation is there for us to build on. We will also begin to give expression to the gifts of spirit that are there so that all of you may have the opportunity of growing nearer to those dear ones who love you so much from the other side of life, and yearn so much to work with you.

With this, I will express my love to you all. Be at peace and keep me in your hearts and in your minds, for I want to hear your thoughts during the time that we are separated. We are separated for two weeks of your time, but I want to be with you during those two weeks. So a thought from you will make it possible for me to link with you.

For now I will say farewell, farewell. God be with you each and every one of you.

Q: I would like to ask about the growing interest in cryonics - the freezing of human corpses in the hope of restoring them to life at some future date. If the body was restored to life in the future, could or would the spirit return?

A: No. As spiritualists know it is a pointless exercise, and people who foolishly part with large sums of money for such a 'service' have no understanding of spirit.

The spirit having departed from its earthly shell and translated to a far superior existence in the spirit world, would certainly have no desire to return to its former 'casing' and life on this inferior plane, and there is NO WAY of inducing it to do so. *

**Concerning the 'Second Coming' of Jesus.*

In his autobiography HAFED A PRINCE OF PERSIA, Hafed says as follows - "He will never appear on the earth again in the body of flesh - here, and now, He appears as our great prince, the sovereign ruler of the worlds of out systems. Not again will He become a child of earth from which He was violently cast forth by cruel men - a martyr for the truth. But, though now ascended to His kingdom, He has still the same love for men - He still compassionates that world which murdered Him, and He still visits you in spirit.

When His second advent is spoken of in your sacred books, it refers to that grand time in your world's future history, when mankind shall be so spiritual, so holy in life, that we who have passed away from earth will be able to communicate face to face with mortal man, and also influence him for good to a far greatest extent than we can now. Then indeed, shall He come - then truly, shall He walk the earth - when His way shall extend from sea to sea, reigning by His truth and love in the hearts of all men.

DISCIPLINE AND FREEDOM

I greet you dear children in the name of love, and in the name of Him who I call Lord and Master. Peace be with each and every one of you.

We have, for some weeks now, been inscribing the law of God on the tablet of your hearts. Whether you know or understand fully what those laws are, doesn't matter at this point in time, for eventually all will be made known and you will be able to stand fast when others might come and try to take away that law that is in your hearts.

I want you all to be very attentive to me, and to the words I give you this afternoon, for perhaps it is going to be the most important set of new values that you are to receive. I tell you that unless you can abide by these new values, you cannot progress. No, not one inch.

I have heard brother Michael say that he doesn't know what direction the circle is taking. The direction, my son, is perhaps not for you to understand, for we have pledged to do the will of God here, and therefore it is His direction that we follow.

At the moment you are likened to young children, still suckling at their mother's breast, and we have greater things to show you and stronger meat for you to eat, but we must first cradle you well, and take you out of the nursery when you can stand upon your own two feet.

Without further to-do, I must go back over the course of these last weeks that we have already listened to, and hopefully learned something. I realise that in many ways they may have been disjointed in your minds, you not being able to piece them together to see where they lead, or exactly what they are teaching you, so I will refresh your minds before we go into the next stage of our discussions.

Can any of you remember the very first time we all came together? Can any of you remember what it was that I said was so important when you take the first step towards God?

A: Honesty?

Hafed: That is so, Honesty. It is a word not to be treated lightly my children, in every aspect of your lives. For the power of honesty is going to help you overcome many things. At the same meeting I also introduced you to someone. Can you remember who that was?

A: We introduced ourselves to God.

Hafed: That is right. Did everyone know this? Or has this just refreshed your minds? Can I hear some voices?

A: Yes, we knew.

Hafed: It is good that you knew this, and even better for those who put it to use. It will serve you no purpose, unless you do.

These things are your servants. They will serve you in the capacity of spiritual growth. After this I spoke to you about the way that Jesus described to those about Him how much God loved them. I told you that He could not in any way use earthly terms, or the wealth of kings to measure the love of God for His children. And as He chose the humble sparrow, and and said to them that that they were worth more than many sparrows, I showed you also how that same sparrow was worth more than the whole world, lock, stock and barrel. How all that which live, and have their being, even in forms of life that you do not recognise as yourselves - such things as the trees in the forest and the flowers in the field, are all God's creation, are all living things, and are all divine.

I said to you that this was a new way of evaluating the true worth of mens' lives. A new door that was opened into another plane of thought, another realm of being. In as much as I did so, further along the pathway that we are taking, I told you about that door, and how you were to pass through it, into that greater light, even while you are here, living on earth.

Many of you said that you could see the door, but you could not pass through, and did not know how to. Of course, since all these things that we have been speaking of are not of physical substance that we can give you to hold in your hands and say, "Look, this is what I mean. This is what a vase is", or "This is a ring", it is very necessary for you to use your minds in purifying your thoughts so that you may harness and channel the spiritual love through that door.

So today, I hope to try and mould for you all these things into a more understandable and acceptable way. In order to do this, I want say to you that we are going to talk upon two words, one is DISCIPLINE and the other is FREEDOM.

Well you know and understand the meaning of those words, for you have only to look and see for yourselves in a dictionary. You understand the need for discipline if one is trying to achieve freedom. But this is the earthly way, and because it is, it is very unsatisfactory for it can be misused on every occasion.

Discipline is to punish for the wrongs of people, and those who have the authority to use that power very often can use it wrongly. They become what I call, power drunk, and use it to achieve their own ends. Or because a child, or someone under their wing is not liked by them. Therefore the punishment does not always fit the crime. It becomes unjust. So discipline by earthly standards is certainly not right.

All must realise the tremendous importance, for can you have freedom without discipline? For you look at your world, and all cry freedom, and all seem to point in different directions as to the way that this freedom is achieved. That is in a global sense - dealing with nations, but there is a more important and urgent way, dealing with the individual. For discipline is to cultivate those finer points within man. Discipline is to help them think aright, and therefore live their life aright.

But freedom my children, is a gift that is also misused. For if you give freedom to them who sit in the spirit of ignorance, they are able to use that freedom to destroy the lives of others, and you have many examples of this in tour world today, especially with your young children who are completely out of control in many ways, who abuse drugs, alcohol, and sex, who rob and steal. All because they have freedom of choice, against the law maybe, but the law has no way of preventing these things.

So you can see just how unsuitable this set of rules are for man to live by, and until he finds and appreciates those higher values, the situation will grow worse than what it is today. So we will try to implant within you, the true meaning of discipline and freedom.

If you look in your scriptures, and one example is the ten commandments, you will read - 'Thou shalt not kill. Thou shalt have no other God. Thou shalt love thy neighbour as thyself. Thou shalt not commit adultery', and these are the laws of God, written that you may establish them in your life. But you do not know how, for within you are frailties of the human body, which very often tempt you away from that which is right, that which is good. And it is like a force within you that you cannot resist, a temptation that you cannot overcome, and so long as you do not know the answers to this, you will never overcome them.

There are many other forms of discipline which are in your life. When you talk about your neighbour or your friend, and run them down with bitter words, or when you allow your tempers to flare, because somebody has called you something, you feel that you must retaliate in the same tongue. You fail when you do this.

But built into the law of God, is the discipline and the freedom. The discipline is found in 'Thou shalt not' - that is the discipline. 'Thus shalt NOT'. For it does not permit you to commit acts that are out of step with God.

The freedom is in the being able to overcome the temptation. So the strength then of the law lies within those words 'Thou shalt not'. To him who has deaf ears and a mind pested with disease of this world, he cannot hear, because there is no feeling. No feelings towards pleasing God. For the way to please God is to keep His laws, and to walk in His love.

There is a great struggle then that goes on within you. For well you know what is right and what is wrong, and well you know that though you may recite the words, it is another matter to put them into practice. For you see, my children, unless your soul is moulded by the discipline of God's laws, then you cannot come to freedom. For the word freedom means that you are no longer challenged by the frailties of the human form. That you have overcome that, and that you have done so through the discipline which 'Thou shalt not' gives to you, for it does not permit you to walk out of step with God.

Coupled with the desire to know and love God, this is the strength that will hold you in check when you are approached by those frailties within you. It will mould your soul into that more perfect being. Each time you overcome, so a greater gift is added to you, that is the gift of spirit. In other words a means by which you can interpret the knowledge of God, because you are closer to God, and you are passing through that door that leads you into that other realm, and you are in harmony with that realm, for you cannot pass through it unless you are, and therefore if there is anything within you that is imperfect, you will not pass through, you cannot pass through, for as I have said to you on other occasions, you cannot take darkness into light.

So this is what your lesson is. This is what you are striving to become. By abiding by the discipline that is in those words, 'Thou shalt not', those holy words, you are growing closer and closer to that freedom that it gives you.

Consider your life now. None of you are free. You are slaves to your weakness and your frailties. You are a slave. And if I say this to you who are spiritually enlightened, what may I say to those whose paths are in darkness, and live in the misery that, that darkness brings?

They too are enslaved, but in a greater way than you. They are enslaved in such a way as they cannot escape. And when they make the change called death, they can only reap the harvest that they have sown, and that is the darkness and misery that has already been imposed upon them.

At first this looks a most unjust law, that they have had nothing but pain and suffering here, and are yet to pass into greater suffering, yes, even to a point where it could cost them their very existence, but it is not the law of God, it is not the desire of God, it is the law that man has made for them, because man does not abide within the love of God, or train his mind to listen to God, or to search God out in the quiet places and have his soul refreshed with peace.

And because he does none of these things, then to the darkness he must go, and the fruit that grows there on those trees are misery and suffering that he must eat, because he had the free will to choose. Because he had freedom without discipline, and therefore no guidance for his mind to avert the dangers that were there lurking in his weakness and his frailties, no strength to overcome temptation.

There is a great sorrow in my heart that I have seen upon the face of the earth, a great ugliness that man does not even recognise, and it is for these dear souls that have lost their way.

Their belief that all the things they sought were bound up in the joy of living, seeking the bright lights, yielding to temptation, and giving themselves to satan himself. Thinking nought about what has been written. Not realising that they are destroying the temple that God has given them, and joins with them in that temple to give them life.

And they make an ugly place of it in their minds, with their filthy thinking, their swear words, and their abuse of drugs and sex. For them that is pleasure, but if you could find a nectar that was sweet to taste, and once swallowed became as a poison to your stomach, then that would be it.

They are blind people, for they can see no further then their desires, their greed, their passions. They are empty people, for no love dwells within them, no true feeling for their mothers and fathers, sisters and brothers, They have bid welcome to the spirit of ignorance to come and dwell within them, and in such a place as that where he lives, it is full of pain.

And when I look around at those who supposedly belong to the Christian religion of your time, and the law of your land, and see no finger raised in opposition to them, no voice that cries out against them, not even anyone to come forward to help them, the Good Samaritan is not abroad in your time. But see them lying in the streets, with their glue-sniffing and their drug-taking, and their alcohol abuse, what kind of mind allows that to continue, and does not speak to put it to an end. Not a spiritual mind, not a mind that knows the truth, but a mind that is just one step ahead of that spirit of ignorance, that pursues them also, And because of it, they can find no peace either by day of by night, because they have forgotten the word of God.

And so then to live by God's values is something entirely different, and we give to you food for thought. Food from heaven that you may indulge yourself in the richness of life that is there to be shared with you.

A freedom that you cannot begin to understand, for no one is your master, and neither are you the master of any, but sit in peace and in love with all God's creation. For until you find that way and pass through that door, you too are deaf and dumb. You too are unable to speak and converse with every form of life.

Therefore my children, it is imperative if you are to go on from here, to think very seriously about what I have said. I know that There are those who will say, 'You cannot live your life like that. We are flesh and blood. We weren't meant to be like that, but I tell you if that is what you think, then flesh and blood you will be and into the darkness you will go.

Because you are spirit here and now, and you have NEVER been flesh and blood, there is no greater time for you than this very moment to put your mind to work, that you may enrich yourselves with that nectar of love which comes from God. That you may be still within yourself, and find that great joy when you come to God who you have been introduced to. A joy which fills your life in such a way, as to give you the strength to resist the temptations, and to heed the discipline of 'Thou shalt not'.

It purifies your thoughts, for no longer do you hunger for things of the flesh. No longer are you compelled to yield yourself to the human form and thus become a slave. For you are not a slave, you were not born to slavery, you were born into freedom that God has given. The free will is yours, but it is your choosing that makes all the difference. The fight, that great war goes on within you, to overcome, to resist, and to be at one with your God.

I know at this particular time in which you live there is great temptation, for the evils of life are strong within man. And you look you see, and you think to yourself, 'This cannot be wrong'. But you do not realise, that anything that takes you away from God, is evil. That is why the first commandment given was 'Thou shalt not' - the discipline that you must rigidly adhere to. 'Thou shalt not have any other God except me', and man has this terrible habit of making Gods at will, and he bows down to his idols of clay, and of gold, and profits nothing from them.

Now I would ask you if you have any questions relating to the discussion that we have had?

No? Good. So then you now know it all, and I have no reason to mention this ever again, and yet I dare say I will do, time and time again.

Now I will take my leave of you, and hope that you have been able to take in all that I have said, and see the importance of it, for it is necessary for you to be able to look at it, and understand it. I realise that try as you will, there will be those occasions when you will slip back and you fail. I do not mind that, and neither do those who minister to you, so long as you are prepared to rise again and to continue the struggle and the fight.

But because I have said this, I would become most annoyed if I found that there are those who use my words to gratify their wrong doing by saying to themselves, 'Oh yes but we are expected to fail, so it doesn't matter', and gives them an excuse, if you will. For if you know this, then you also know the discipline that says 'Thou shalt not'. To fail is one thing, but to use it as an excuse, is completely different.

I will bid you farewell, and take my leave of you all until we assemble again on another one of your days. Live in peace, go in peace, and love your neighbour as yourself. Goodnight and God bless you.

THE PRODUCT OF OUR USE OF TIME

Moments tick away, and we hardly recognise that they have departed from our life. We know not how we have spent them, either in thought or in action, and yet each moment that slips away, amounts to hours and days and yet years, and much of mans' life is allowed to slip by in this unseemly way, this unfashionable way. For it is not creative, it is not loving. It is like a vacuum.

Every now and again we suddenly come alive and spring into action, and begin to do something with our life, whether it is in work or in play, or whether it is in coming to the knowledge of God. Then we seem to slip back again, into the old pattern of life where moments go by, and nothing worthwhile is produced from that time.

My children, when you come to our other side of life, you will, in viewing your life again, find that much of your life was spent in this non-productive way. Doing nothing and thinking nothing that is of a creative nature. You will discover that you have let a good part of your life pass by, that could have been put to much better and creative use.

It is also said that an idle mind creates idle thoughts, and those who do not keep check of their thoughts or of their mind, soon fall into a state of repair and allow all unfashionable thoughts to enter into their minds. Thoughts which are not in any way profitable to their owner, for they can be of a destructive nature, especially if they carry with them the seed of jealousy, and especially if they carry those feelings of hatred. All of this is the poison that does not only affect your physical body, but affects your spiritual body as well.

For while the tongue is a little member of your body, and speaks great things or small things it is your mind that gives your tongue utterances of those words. Therefore you will see how very important it is, to control your thoughts and to build the strength of your thinking power along the lines of love and peace. Even though at times you may be put to the test by others around you, who do and say things that give you great annoyance and cause great anger to begin to rise within you.

And these things are the weaknesses my children that you must overcome, for anything that is ugly or of an ugly nature, will surely affect your etheric body and transform it, not into that beauty, but into the ugliness that it marks it with. For well you have heard the saying 'As ugly as sin', and surely that is for all of you to take note of.

For the ugliness of that sin, to who performs it, marks the soul, and it is the soul that becomes ugly, and not only that, but it will eventually transform the look of peoples faces and in their eyes. shines through, just as the brightness of God shines through those who have a saintly look.

So does then, hatefulness change the look on your face and the look in your eyes, for when the light of compassion has gone from your eyes, then what is there left but a blank expression of self, of hate, or jealousy and greed. A mixture that can perform terrible hurt to others and to yourself.

I want to, if I can possibly put it into words, to show you how the body that you wear, does not in any way represent the soul that you are. It is true to say, that when you make the change called death, you will carry the same likeness of the body that you wear now, but there will be a marked difference. For those who have tried to live their life in pleasing God, they will find that there is a different kind of beauty. A beauty that is alight within them. A great softness, gentleness, all of which are the very essence of your soul, and are shown by that spiritual reflection upon your face.

I know that it is foolish of me to try and express myself in this way when you have not in any way seen, or are able to comprehend just what I am speaking about, but it is written that you are all in the likeness of God, and that is true, but it is not in the likeness of the flesh, for the flesh will decay and remain here - it is the likeness of the spirit that burns within you. That spirit is what God is, for God is spirit, and you cannot expect spirit to be, in any shape or form, likened to flesh. It is a very poor comparison, for it is a totally different substance, totally different in every way.

Only when you come to see this for yourself, will you begin to understand. When your spirit eyes are opened, in that world that is yet to come for you, you will then see how all those that you knew and loved here, on earth, have a kind of lustre about them, that you have never ever seen before. A shining gentleness that is filled with compassion and love.

Now, this my children, is how you are going to grow, and each time your thoughts become enlightened by the power of truth, so then does that lustre begin to shine through and changes your face, and changes your nature, and you can see the reflection of your soul through your eyes, for they have that sympathy and that love and sincerity within them, and your face is one that carries the mark of that spirituality, which says, 'I am a child of God', for that is what you are all coming to be, the children of God.

You see things totally different when this is beginning to happen, and I am sure that, yes, you who are here, have noticed this, that through your mind, and the light that it carries, you see things differently, you understand them differently. Your way of life, your way of thinking, has totally changed, and it is no longer you as the individual, but you as one of the family of God.

And your heart goes out to all those who are less fortunate than yourself, and you try hard to put that spiritual virtue within all of your brothers and sisters that are here, and yet cannot. Because at this point in time they have yet to reach that spiritual level where they can accept with their heart and mind, the truth that you have laboured so earnestly to bring them.

They are still bogged down in the worldly things. They still look to the pleasures of earth to satisfy and gratify the needs of their physical body. Well you know how wrong it is, and how much suffering and pain it will bring, not only to them, but to others who they inflict it on, And yet still they cannot change the course of their life, for they are not ready to receive what you have.

And you must see and know that there are many such souls in your world today, but do not be despondent, for there are many, many, many souls, who are right on the border-line, who are questioning in their hearts and minds, as to who they are, what they are, and is there really a God, and what are they DOING here? Is what they see about them right? Can pain be the answer to their life? Can tears, hunger and disease be the only joy and happiness they can find?

They are waiting for people like yourself, who come along with that bread of heaven and give to them a few morsels from the Lord's table, and that is enough to spark off their soul with enthusiasm.

They think, 'I have heard something today that is different. What is it? What does it mean? There seems to be something in there that is truth. Something that I really want to understand', and that is their first introduction to truth, and their God, and then you say to them "Ah, listen brother, I would like to introduce you to your heavenly Father through prayer", and they begin to recognise that they can have a perfect union with their God through prayer by entering into the silence of their mind and being still, and saying "Father it is John, it is Doris, it is Maureen. I have come to ask for your blessing. I have come to ask for your forgiveness", knowing always that as surely as you have asked, so shall He bless you, so shall He forgive you.

It is not the blessing of worldly things, you understand. It is not even perhaps the blessing that heals your body, or one who you love, but it is the blessing that has great power within it. It enters your heart and mind, and sets afire a great yearning within you, to know of His love, and to be protected by His truth, and shielded from the frailties of the human body that you still wear, to imagine that in an instant of time you could give way to one of them, and because of it, your whole life is desecrated. Father, please protect me from myself.

And in a little while, like you, they too become conscious of wanting to do something to repay Him. Wanting to be of service to Him. And yet at that stage they are still blind. They are blind because their spiritual eyes are yet to open. Yes, they have all the yearning within them, they want to be another disciple, go and cry out His name in the streets. For their love and compassion for their fellow man grows in the same proportion as their love for God grows, and they cannot hold it back, and yet they cannot express themselves, for all of this is tied up within them, because their tongue cannot give utterance to a feeling that has not yet been processed by the mind into words.

Yet like you, little by little, they become ever more conscious of those from the realms of light, those who are the Father's ambassadors of love. He sends them forth saying, "Look, seek out my little ones, and teach them of Me, and fill them with that comfort, the food from heaven that they need, and say to them - Yes, if you earnestly desire to give service to your brother then those spiritual gifts shall be yours.

So it is that as we, you and I, sit here now, there is a great noise within heaven all about us. A great noise from those who come from the realm of light, to tend to the little ones of God, to fill them up with good thoughts, with the good meaning of life, with the positive hope of life which you are feeling now. It is passing through you now and you are experiencing the beginning of that touch that is of God. It is awakening your soul to who you are, and saying to you 'Look - fear not, for there is nothing to fear. For what if death should come to you, life is an endless journey, and back home you will come".

And he who keeps watch on the city gates, shall cry out "Lord, Master, him who you have sent about your business, even now stands at the city gates". Remember, remember those words, and He will send to you His servants, to dress you in the right apparel, in those spiritual garbs that you have earned for yourself as a right. And among them will be those who have ministered to you while you have sat here preparing to take on the tools of the spirit that you might give greater service to all about you, and they come to minister their love to you, and all of those who you have helped, given those morsels of holy bread from the Lord's table, they are here too, giving you their love, that your wealth may have no end.

And when you look through those eyes of the spirit, with this more perfect understanding and assurance of God, you will see so much more. You will know so much more. You will no longer ask, how does God prophecy the events which are to come, for you will know. With your mind crystal clear, and perfected into that spiritual child, you will see most clearly the events which are yet to come.

Yet you are here now, preparing for the journey to come, and I speak not of the journey that is to take you into the higher life when you are to pass from here, when you are no longer with me, no longer with your brothers and sisters who sit about you, but you are on your own, and you go forward on that path of service to show that you were made of the right metal.

On that Journey you shall meet many others who come to you and ask for your help, for your healing, for your prayers, for they will believe and it will be so, that God hears you more than them.

And your eyes will be open, to give that message of comfort from their loved ones and friends, and your eyes will be open in order to give that message of truth that will spur them on.

But you yourself will find obstacles in your way, for no path of service is easy, especially when you go forth alone, for there is always that little bit of doubt that is in you. Always that feeling that maybe no one will come to stand up and give that truth as it has been given you. Perhaps when you do to one who is in need and says to you, if not in words but in feeling, "Help me, help me", you may not know how to help.

But these things are always there to challenge you, for if the challenge was not there, then what good would it all be, for always on every occasion, you have got to prove yourself to your God, that in spite of your own doubts and fears, you go forth and present yourself, knowing that the work is done in and through you, but never by you.

And if your faith and courage is such, then you will never ever be left alone, you will never be let down, for those who love you, who come to walk 'in your life with you, will always be there, although as many times as that happens, it will never ever clear away that doubt, and that fear, before you take a service, before you do the healing, wherever it is you must work for God. That will always be there, for it is the challenge for you, to see whether you have the courage and the faith to stand up for your God.

Now I will leave you. Farewell, farewell.

LIVING ACCORDING TO THE LAW

My children, for this long time now I have been endeavouring, with others, to inject in you something of those greater values in life, which are to be found in the spiritual versions of life. Something of the laws of God, and had you been listening to the reading that was given (John 15, v 12-27), you would have found a great deal within them about the laws of God.

Well you know that I have spoken on many different matters over past weeks, relating to this truth that must inspire and guide each one of you, realising that nothing of course, will happen, unless you yourselves are prepared to put it into your lives, and live your lives according to that law, you have a greater life to come. One which makes the life that you have at present, very dim, very dingy. A life that is filled with unmeasurable joy of many different experiences that are there, and those experiences being set free from fears, doubts, and anything which is ugly or painful.

We realise that much of what we have said relating to this path that we wish you to walk, has been difficult for you to comprehend. Difficult indeed, to see and believe in that life that is filled with those treasures that you will never find here. For mans' determination to proceed with his life along his own particular way, which is basically seeking out for himself and himself alone, does not give him anything which is of true value. Even though he may succeed several times over, he is still the loser in the long run.

You have a saying in your life, which says, 'You mustn't mix politics with religion', I of course, cannot in any way divulge to you the truths that I have, without being involved in the politics of your lives, or of the world, for they, in many ways, are in opposition to the will of God, and the laws of God, and God WILL have His way.

Laws are made at the present time by Parliament, of which few people take notice. Even fewer consider where these laws will land them in the future. All these laws seem to be set to one end - for the profit of him who has most, and for the downfall of him who has least.

I wish to make some comparisons, in order to show you the two different ways of life. Well you know something of the immense force that has presented law after law according to Parliament, that has not been to the good of the common people. Indeed, it has caused much heartache, it has caused much suffering.

There are more people, for example, who do not have a place to dwell, they live on the streets. There are more people who have no work at all, because it is seen that by the greater numbers unemployed, the less money there is to purchase the goods in the shops, and thus create inflation. So therefore, if the money is not available to purchase those items inflation comes down. But at whose expense? Only at the expense of the working man.

There are those other things which deal with your hospitals. Your health service, which well you know is conformed along the lines of: Those who have most, receive most. It is good for the man who has the money to pay, but little hope for the man who has not.

All these things have been changed you see, since there has been a change of Government. There is also the heavy burden that has been placed upon the poor and lifted from the rich regarding poll tax, and many other things, and because there has been a great bargain sale of all national industries, the prices have risen very sharply, and the poorer man cannot find the money to pay.

There is also an attack upon the old, and even those who will one day be pensioners themselves. For indeed, at this time, you who are young must ferret to purchase some kind of insurance which will support you in your old age. When those who at the present time are also too old to have that kind of policy, they live off the state. Not something that the state gives them, but what they have paid for throughout their working lives. But when the present generation have faded away and gone, those who remain, will be left to their own devices to provide for their old age. But then if you are unemployed and you cannot afford to live, as it is now, where do you find the money to purchase that kind of security? What will happen when those same people arrive at the door of old age? Where does their money come from?

So you see, the laws that are made are not for the average man, but always for the rich. Children too have been affected since schools have also had their money reduced. All of it you see, is not conducive to the laws of God.

I am not in any way advocating a Labour Government, or any other hind of Government. I have no doubt that there are weaknesses in all the parties, for man and his frailties are in every way part of the pattern of his life.

Is this way that God wants His children to live? I want you to remember that God has said that all His children are equal, and you are all His children. Because you are all equal, you are all part of the life that He has given to you, and no man should be treated differently from another, regardless of his colour or his religion. All should be equal.

Take note also that God did not provide land solely for those who are wealthy. By what right do they have that land? I realise that it is a system of laws that have grown up with generation after generation, and has brought man to the stage where he lives according to these laws, but they are non-theless unjust laws. They are not laws of God's making, and I have said to you that God WILL have His way.

Many, many years ago, and perhaps there are some here now who can recall, I said that the foundation of Communism was beginning to crack. That one day it would fall, and that the great wall in Germany would fall. At the time I mentioned these things, there was no indication whatsoever of these things ever happening, and yet overnight it would seem, these things took place, because God knew that in order to bring His laws into being, He must remove these objects. Because they were contrary to His law. And it was done.

At that time I also said that there would come a time when the finances of man and the God that he worshipped would also fall and be no more. For the laws of God do not make way for money to be part of mans' life. It is not a good thing to build upon, for it encourages the greedy and it denies the poor their rights.

It has always been, therefore, God's intention to bring this world to that point of spiritual understanding where He may introduce His laws into your lives. Laws which state in the Bible 'Thou shalt not steal', 'Thou shalt honour thy mother and father', 'Thou shalt not commit adultery', 'Thou shalt not kill', 'Thou shalt have only one God'. We realise that man already has these, but he breaks them, because today he cannot see any purpose in not doing so, and yet it has taken thousands of years for man to come to this point in time when he is becoming more conscious of help for the needy.

Indeed, you have seen something of this with the poorer nations who have been in poverty and starving. You have seen it with the victims of war, and even now in Russia. But at all times, man has wanted something in return. He was looking for profit, either in the form of money, land, trading rights. There was nothing that was given with a good spiritual heart - without strings attached.

God it is who supplies all the needs for man. True it is that man must go and work in order to bring these things into being. Even so, he may work as hard as he wishes and as long as he wishes, but nothing would come unless it was granted by God. That is to say, all the food that you eat, and all the materials that make your world what it is. Therefore, man has prospered and gone along the path of materialism a lot faster than he has the path of spirit and spirituality.

There must be a balancing of these things, for you cannot travel along the path of materialism without taking into account the spirituality that is required by each one in order to keep a balance of things in the world, and to uphold justice for all mankind. God has ever been mindful of these things, and over the course of time has been working wards bringing that light of salvation to His children, and implanting within their minds the laws and the truth of those laws that give real justice.

And so you have witnessed over the course of your small lives, something of the workings of God, hidden from man, and yet made manifest. You have begun to see the change that is coming to the world, and all these events are to happen if the world is to become as God intended.

There are still obstacles that have yet to be removed. For other nations have roots within them of hatred, poisoned by the years that have passed between their nation and others. They too are growing with wealth, and growing in unity, which is something that did not happen before. In the Eastern countries there was always division in the Arab world, but now that is slowly beginning to change, although the old hatreds remain.

In the next four to five years, you are to witness and see great events which are to change your world still further. Much of that will not be to mans' liking, but it will be mans' inhumanity that will inflict it on others. At the same time, it will become as a lesson for the future generations, because always out of turmoil and suffering something new is born. Like a woman who gives birth to a child, suffers the pain of birth, and yet, out of it comes a son or daughter, that gives to her great joy and fills her heart with a new kind of peace. So it is with the world at large, that out of mans' future suffering shall be born a new age which holds in its folds many of the laws that God has always intended man to live by. Men then will be ready and willing to grasp at those laws, live by them, and be at peace with each other.

Do not forget the prophecies of Jesus. For He said, 'Blessed are the meek, for they shall inherit the earth'. And so shall it be. There will be a new form of life born to all, and it will not depend on wealth, ambition, greed, and the status of one country over another. Neither will it be according to the rulers of the land, for a new spirit will enter man. It will be the spirit of God, and truly it will cry, "Abba, Father:" And truly man will rule himself, according to that spirit within.

As I have said that God is the provider of all the needs of man, so too will that become very clear. Not like today, where man in his greed takes great pride in possessing more than he needs, and thus drains the world of its resources, but rather, my children, shall it be that man will take only his needs. For that indwelling spirit that is God, will teach him that by the bread of faith, peace and love he has been fed. Out of that comes his joy of living. Living in a world that is free from disease, free from brutal violence of every description. Peace shall rule the land, and joy shall visit the hearts of all men.

All men will work for each other. For in that time it will be possible. No man will lay aside more than he needs, or accuse his neighbour of not working harder than himself. All men will be united in that spirit of God. The council of God shall rule the hearts of all men, and He who we call Lord and Master shall truly be your King. The world that you have now shall be no more, but shall have changed and gone away.

You, my children who sit here, may say to yourselves, "What of us? For if this turmoil is to happen, will our lives be taken in that turmoil?".

I say to you, 'Ten thousand may fall at your right side, and ten thousand may fall at your left side, but it shall not come unto thee, for I am with you, sayeth the Lord'.

If any of you shall make the change called death, it shall be natural. It shall be because it is the time, whether it is through disease or accident, it is the time. You will come to us and be one of the many, many legions of Christ's soldiers, who come in that hour to bring an end to the terrible violence that happens then.

I tell you these things, not to frighten you, not to make you full of fear, for that is not the purpose. But there is a saying, that to be forewarned is to be forearmed. That is why. It is to show to you who are gathered here, the great importance of the work that the Master calls you to do. This is why we say you must change. You must become a new creature. You must let the old creature die. For that belonged to yesterday.

You belong to tomorrow. You belong to the new world. You belong to 'A new set of values'. A new set of laws which will govern over you. You have work to do in all this. So draw yourselves from fear, for fear is your enemy, and always has been.

Fill yourselves with that courage and strength that comes from God, in the truth of God. You must bind yourselves together in true friendship and love, and on another occasion I am going to deal with this, to make you conscious of your duty towards God, yourselves, and those who assemble here each week.

So my children, the time has come for me to say farewell. Hopefully you have listened to all that I have said, and absorbed it. I realise that it has raised many questions in your minds, but be patient for now. I cannot reveal more than I have told you at this time, so you must be patient.

Good afternoon, and God bless each one of you.

THOU SHALT LOVE THY NEIGHBOUR AS THYSELF

Good afternoon and God bless you, my children.

And so it is written - Except your goodness is greater than the Pharisees, you shall not enter the kingdom of heaven.

Many there are who say to me, "That is not so, for when you make the change called death you are in the kingdom of heaven". They believe, wrongly, that the spirit spheres are the kingdom of heaven, and of course it is not so.

The kingdom of heaven is the ultimate goal that you have, and there are seven spheres for you to travel through before you approach that. Yet there are those who gather on earth, and have done so since the beginning of time, who, when making that change called death, enter into that kingdom of heaven. For they are those souls who give up their places especially to come here to teach their brother and help their brother both with words of light and truth and guidance, that they may not continuously go astray and thus into the poverty of the soul, but go towards the light that shines from the kingdom of heaven. Such as these, give up much in order to come here and do just this.

I know that many times I have said to you - regarding those souls in other spheres in the universe whose life is totally different from yours, that you cannot begin to understand what their life is like, indeed you would probably think it must be extremely boring. For you need entertainment of different kinds to fill your lives with some kind of purpose and excitement. But there are those in that other sphere of life, far removed from the way that you live, who would not dream of doing or even searching for that kind of entertainment. Boredom does not come to them, for it is just a weakness of man. A weakness that, yet again, he must learn to overcome. In good time, he will do this.

These other souls are steadfast in the ways of peace and love, and their way of life is filled with joy and pleasure, through the existence that they have, and existence that I could not begin to explain, for there are no words which I could say to you that would explain it.

Why do you think I keep reminding you, and bringing this picture to you? Have you any idea of the reason why I do this?
A: To encourage us, and to make us think beyond what is in front of us right now.
Hafed: Yes. That is quite so. It is to show you the difference and the distance of the journey you undertake in order to go back home. It is a vision I place in your hearts, not only for you to see the difference that lies between you, but hopefully to inspire hope within you all.

It was never placed there for you to grow despondent at the journey that still lies ahead. I know that the donkey who cannot see the carrot refuses to walk, but in you the journey is always removed, and hope always flows freely. Yes, despair will surely be thrown across your path, in which you become enmeshed and held back. There are many of those from the lower realms who wish to put your journey at an end, but God who loves you all, calls to His faithful, and leaves you not alone. He sends forth His angels of light to give you that inner strength to lift yourselves up and raise your minds above the earthly things, that you may see the vision anew, to refresh your souls.

In this sense my children, we gather together each week, you and I, along this earthly path, and I as your teacher, wish you to know that I come to you at the command of Him whom I call Lord and Master, and who loves you. I tell you this not to grow in importance in your eyes, for that is wrong. I tell you this that you might grow to trust my words and know, that because they are not mine they are true. They are filled with that promise that is held for each and every one of you.

There must surely come a time when you must stand as one of the servants of God, and preach the truth before your fellow men. In order to do this, you must know what the truth is, and you must also grow in spiritual stature within yourselves, that no challenge from the lower realms can defeat your purpose, and cause you to fall. No frailty within you, no roots can rise up and blind you to the truth. No temptation can stand before you and defeat you.

All these things at the moment, are there within you, my children. And so, little by little, I teach you in that hope, that express and desired hope, that you may free yourselves from all that which holds you fast to the earth.

So it is, that this afternoon, I would like to talk about one of the commandments. That commandment is - Thou shalt' love thy neighbour as thyself.

I would ask you for your explanation, even though it may appear to explain itself. But what do you think? What do you feel? Thou shalt love thy neighbour as thyself. Would any of you care to voice an opinion on this?

A: To be in harmony with one another. To understand one another, even when being provoked. To be diplomatic in all that you do. To come together in peace.

A: To treat everyone with whom you come in contact with, the same way that you would want to be treated yourself. Not how you ARE treated, but how you would want to be treated.
A: I would say it is being able to put yourself in their shoes, and see things from their point of view, so that you truly understood them.
Hafed: Anyone else? No? Well, all these things that you have said are just and true, and yet there is more to be seen, more to be known.

Perhaps what I am going to say, you will think - "Who can do this?" It is something which I realise cannot be done in the world as a whole, yet still it is for you to make it your goal, for it embraces many of the qualities of the spirit of God, that He has given to His children that they might unfold as they grow nearer in that spiritual wisdom, to Him.

The prophet Mohammed gave a more explicit answer to the commandment 'Thou shalt love thy neighbour as thyself'. They were not just intended to be words for you to know the meaning of. They were meant to be practiced fully in your lives

For to love thy neighbour as thyself, means to share all your life with him. It means to give to him the same as you would hope he would give to you. To share the same bread. That whatever he does not have, you would share with him. You would share your food and your water and your home. You would give him your love.

Now I realise that in this world that you have, it cannot be so, because the law of man has made it impossible for that to happen. But it does not mean to say that your heart must be unclean, because of the laws of man. But rather that the truth should purify your heart, that you may see that your brother is equal to you in every way. That you may do whatever you can to help his plight. Not just simply to guide him in the truth that God has given you, but also be prepared to share what you have with him.

It is therefore a question that you must reach that spiritual love which makes this possible. If you were to say these things to people, they would laugh at you. They would perhaps, say cruel things, for they do not understand. But when we talk about the kingdom of heaven, these are the qualities of the soul that you need to grow towards, then indeed you will know that you are on the path to heaven.

It is not something that is bound up in words. It is much, much more than this. It is a feeling of being at one with your brother, It is a spiritual link, a spiritual bond, that cannot be broken.

For you, my children, we put them who are lesser than you, and weaker than you, in your care, for you to help. For the very poorest man, through possessing the zeal of God, will be the richest among those who have such, and yet have nothing. For they do not know God.

You are coming to that awakening, where you are able to feel and understand something of the greatness of God's love. You have a long way yet to go to fulfill that love completely, within you. When it is so, when it has come, then you will understand fully why that way of life that others live in the spheres far removed from you, do so with the greatest of joy, and the greatest of pleasure. For they are free from the daily toil that you rush to each morning. They are freed from the ambition of achieving things in the worldly sense. They are freed from the worry of financial troubles, they have none of these. Neither do they have the obsession that the drug-taker has, or the loose women have, or the gambler or the drinker. They are freed from all these obsessions.

It is not for you to look down on such people, for you must remember that they are your neighbours, and these are the weaker ones whom God has referred to you. Therefore, you must help in whatever way you can, even if it is only by remembering them in your prayers, and enfolding them in your love. For they must, in time, grow from that anxiety into the light.

Mans' ignorance has created a way of life that has ensnared his children, and brought them to great suffering and great pain, because of those in the lower realms, who were likened to them when they lived here, and who increase that obsession by bringing to them that craving. As they must strive to free themselves from that desire of life, so you must do what you can to aid them.

Think not to yourself that you are freed from this, for you are not. You have perhaps, lesser frailties than they, but lacking care you too could fall into the snare. For if angels can fall from grace, cannot you? I would think so.

So you must always be on your guard against your frailties and your thoughts, for not always are they yours, but rather are they being moulded and created as a pitfall for you by those in the lower realms.

So my children, you will begin to see the fight that is there, and how you must raise up this zeal of God within you, and fortify yourselves with His love and with the knowledge that wisdom brings. Above all, the desire to walk in God's laws.

Here you are, gathered together in this sanctuary of light, of love, and healing, which we constantly replenish and repair, and where we bring that peace that you might come and sit at your Father's footstall, and feel His presence.

You all have a duty towards each other. Just like you have towards your neighbour. You must realise how you can cause the downfall of your brother, or sister, who sits here. For it depends, you see, how you are prepared to live your lives. How you are willing to give yourselves to God.

You must look at each other, and love each other a great deal more than you do now, my children. Your concern for each other must be as for your own. That is what love is, and that is what we are trying to raise up within you, to say nothing of those qualities of Christ,

If there is one among you who thinks wrongly of another, then you must go to your God and ask not only for His forgiveness, but to cast that thought from your mind. For that is the door through which those of the lower realms may enter and destroy this temple of light.

My son's life (Douglas Arnold), is always at stake, I want you to realise this. For it is he who they really want to bring down. Without him, you can no longer prosper. Through him, the teachers of Christ come, and none can enter to destroy him, for my Lord would not allow it. He would not permit it.

It is for you my children, that I bring these things forward, and speak to you of the deep things that are in the law of God. I show to you that if you cannot do these things one towards the other, how are you to do them towards those whom you do not know? It is from small acorns that great oak trees grow, and you are small acorns that we are planting in the vineyard of God, that you may grow and give shelter to all men. Though you are few in number, your truth will grow in the hearts of many, and that truth will enter into your minds and hearts and fill your mouths with those gracious words that come from God.

I tell you no lies, my children, when I tell you that your holy Father is no longer prepared to accept the ways of man, and His will WILL be done, here on earth. Already He is taking down the temples that man has built, brick by brick. If they will not listen, then He will leave them desolate. You have evidence of this already, for you see that those nations who were strong and great have fallen. The bricks of their great temples of philosophy have been removed. You see it happening all through Europe and Russia.

Because He has chosen to do this with them, with their so-called Communist regime, it does not mean to say that He favours the ways of the West, the North, or the South.

It is His intention to put His laws in the hearts and minds of every nation, that every nation may live by those laws and they truly know that - 'Thou shalt have no other God before Me', 'Thou shalt not kill', 'Thou shalt take nothing of thy neighbour's'.

Man will come to understand, and will come to live by these laws, for in his heart will come that new idea of life, that new hope that will fashion his thinking. He will no longer desire to own much, rather share much. No longer desire to receive much, but to give much. No longer be prepared to waste his life on idle things where the devil has his way, but to spend his life in the enjoyment of knowing his brother and his God, creating an existence where all work together to give to each other.

Those who spend their lives in pursuit of ownership, desiring to own big houses, big firms, lots of land, and much money, will suddenly come to the knowledge of what Jesus said - "What shall it profit a man to gain the whole world, and lose your very own soul". They will suddenly come to realise how empty and dead all their works have become. For they have profited nothing.

It will be as though they have been in a trance, and have gathered to themselves all the dust of the earth, and piled it up and worshipped it and protected it. Then they wake and see the squalor that they are sitting in.

Your gold and your treasure will be each other. Your contentment and your happiness will be in the full knowledge of the joy that comes from your brother, and that great inner yearning to please each other, and to please your God.

Blessed are they that are pure in heart, for they shall see our God. Blessed are the meek for they shall inherit the earth.

You will know the true meaning of all this, and you will see its true purpose come alive, like a newness of spirit that will fill you with a new ambition, new dream, new hopes. You will want to tie your souls to the will of the Lord, that you may travel with Him, where 'ere He may go.

I hope that I have been able to plant a few seeds in your minds, that will grow up and be fruitful in times to come. That you may clearly understand that which we began to speak of from the beginning, about those higher set of values, and just what they mean.

Farewell beloved, farewell. I journey a little way from you, but only a little way, and always we are there with you.

QUALITIES OF FAITH

Good afternoon my children, I greet you in the name of love, and in the name of Him whom I call Lord and Master. Peace be with each and every one of you.

As I have said many times, it is always our privilege to come and address you in this sweet way, for I come not on my own, but travel with many other dear souls who join me here on your behalf, that during the course of your lesson they may draw near to you and open your minds, that you may understand to some degree the lesson at hand.

Today my children, I want to continue in that phase of the higher awareness that we began, a new set of values. For there is so much in your scriptures that man does not fully understand, and indeed can never understand until he begins to hear the truth from the teachers in spirit, who alone, have the key to open out greater depths of feeling and vision for him.

We talk about faith, you and I, on many, many occasions, and I wonder at times whether you truly understand about faith, and what faith is. To many it is a belief in God, and of course, I suppose this is fundamentally true, and yet it is so much more than just that.

Jesus says, "What is faith? If you had faith such as a mustard seed, then you would be able to tell the mountain - henceforth be cast into the sea - and it would obey you". It seems to me then, that surely those of you who think about faith, and think to yourselves that you have faith, must realise that there is so much more to the quality of faith that Jesus speaks of, than the quality of faith that you have.

Many people say they believe in God, and yet spend their lives doing everything that is against Him. Many people say they believe in God and have faith, but when trouble comes knocking at their door, their faith flies out of the window. Soon they find that this God they had such faith in disappoints them, for how could He allow these things to happen to them?

Faith then, is something more than that quality which they hold. Faith must endure against the storms of life, and hold you in a stable position where you may still say "I believe in God".

To achieve that special quality of faith, the knowledge of God must be deep within you. It cannot just simply be there because you want it to be true, for that is not good enough. While we speak about faith, one to the other, there is something even more than faith. For always when you say "I believe" there is a question mark which says I believe in God, yet how deep is that belief, how strong is that faith?"

It usually depends on whether the sun is shinning in their life, or whether it is stormy. For like I have said, when they are put to the test, God seems to fly from them, and they accuse Him, or deny Him.

Those of you who go a step further and say "I don't have faith in God, I KNOW that there is a God", this is a much stronger belief. It is a belief that cannot be shaken, regardless of what happens. It says I KNOW there is a God", and though all kind of troubles may come my way, even though I may feel hurt and think that God has forsaken me, all these things can I think and realise, but I will never say "God does not exist".

Once you know that God IS, and does exist, then you can never again disbelieve that He IS God, creator of all life. That is the next step forward. It brings you into that standard or strength that you cannot in any way disprove God, or say He doesn't exist.

None of these qualities of faith will produce for you the casting of the mountain into the sea. So what do we say? Do we say then, that the words of Jesus are false? That it cannot be? Or do we say that there is another step forward to a greater faith than we have now? Faith is a quality, a substance, a knowing, and it holds you in good stead in life. We know all of this. So what more is there, than that faith that we possess?

There is a gulf that lies between the quality of faith that you possess, and the quality of faith that Jesus speaks of, and you must bridge that gulf with other qualities of the spirit as you go on through life, day by day. The two faiths are not of the same standard. For example, you would not expect to pay the same price for imitation silk, that you would pay for real silk, would you? That is the difference between the two faiths - the one that Jesus speaks of, and the one that you have, which is an inferior faith. What it must now need, is to be strengthened. It has to be strengthened in a way - not with more belief, for if you already know that God exists, then you can strengthen it more than that, but it needs to have within its folds, other qualities of the soul. Those spiritual qualities that I have often spoken of to you.

They are qualities of meekness and gentleness, love and humility, forgiveness and understanding. Each one of them is a spiritual quality, a substance. They are going to build your bridge for you. The bridge that you must span across from one faith to the other. They are not only going to do this, they are going to bring you to that point where you are no longer the children of God, but the sons and daughters of God. For these are those other spiritual qualities that you must build within your souls, and raise them up so that you become complete.

If you look at those qualities that I have spoken of, you will discover that each one of them is a quality of a creative nature. They have the power to create.

If you think about humility, that virtue that comes to you and makes you less high minded, less of a braggart, more sincere, more humble, it is a strong quality, for no one can serve God unless they are humble. It is a fundamental strength that you need in order to build a foundation upon, that foundation of the soul that is to become the sons or daughter of God.

If you look at the quality of forgiveness, here again is another creative energy. An energy that creates for good, just like humility creates for good. It is not a destructive element. It is a creative element that enriches your soul, and brings to you that greater awareness of who you are.

You look at love, another creative energy. It brings into your life, and into the lives of others, happiness and joy. It does not have any destructive element.

All these are the qualities that you need, in order to grow and span that gulf that lies between you and those sons and daughters of God, where you will have that faith such as a mustard seed - Because when you have accomplished all these things, when you have received those spiritual gifts to the degree that they are constantly with you, they are your armour against the frailties and the temptations of life. They rid you of all thoughts that are of a destructive nature, thoughts which are not necessarily evil, but which are not good - where you think and speak ill of people without really knowing, because you feel a little spiteful towards them, or because you are jealous of them.

You see, if those same qualities of love and humility and understanding are in you, you cannot have those frailties of spitefulness, jealousy and hatred. They would have long gone.

So you see there is a vast challenge that lies before you all. The more you become aware of these things, the more that you open yourself out to learning about them, then the wiser you are and the greater your gifts, until you reach that point where miracles are possible through you. Then are you capable of allowing the God creative spirit to flow through you, and do whatever is necessary.

You lay your hands on a sick person now - hopefully they will respond and sometimes they do, but if it is that you are looking for instant healing - miracles, then it has to be with that flow of Godpower, through you. That can only be done when those other spiritual flowers have been raised up in your minds and your hearts, and you are capable of putting them to use and allowing yourselves to be used by that holy power of God which cannot flow through an instrument which is imperfect. It cannot be done. It would be like trying to get a light from your electricity without using a bulb. The power comes so far down, and then stops.

This is where the pitfalls begin. It is in the awareness of life, the physical nature that you have fights against the spiritual nature that is really you. The struggle is there always, because one is yearning for the worldly things, and the other for the spiritual things, depending upon what is in your nature. You are here to rise above that nature, and overcome it, and there you may see where the struggle lies.

It is no good saying to yourself - "Oh, it is too strong for me. I cannot do it". You can. This you see, is the awakening that comes when you have built your bridge across that gulf that lies between your faith and the faith 'that Jesus speaks of. It is the awakening OF YOU, Not saying "It can't be done, I can't do it", but knowing that you CAN do it. Being over conscious that you must motivate things with the power of your mind. Because your mind has been allowed to grow in that spiritual way which holds that creative energy, then you must put it to use. Don't say or even think that it cannot be done, for to say that is to say that God can't do it, and this is what you are asking. You are asking God to do it. Not you.

In as much as you are asking God to do this, you are now aware and conscious of what role you are to play - if God is to be able to do it. Allowing His power to be channelled through you.

When such things as Jesus did in His life, were done - walking on water, and producing food from out of nowhere, all these things were done by that power of God flowing through Him. It was the manipulation of the conditions around Him that made those conditions bend to the will of God.

Could you imagine walking, upon water? Of course you can't, it is beyond you even to understand it. And yet, done it was. Done by the right strength of thought. By believing that with God all things are possible, and allowing His power, that creative energy, to change the laws of the physical nature on earth to the will of God. And it was done.

Many, many times it is done. You see it in instant healing, where those who are pronounced beyond help by the medical profession, suddenly rise up and are made whole. They are so, because the very conditions of that illness have been changed. Into them came a creative energy of life that renewed those parts that were diseased.

These things are what you must get into your minds, as you are approaching those qualities of meekness, gentleness, love and understanding. It is these qualities that blend the forces of nature with the forces of God and make these things happen. You don't have to understand HOW it is done. You just have to have the ability to say that it CAN happen.

As I began in the beginning, by telling you that the next step forward from faith was 'I know that God exists"- 'I KNOW', and that is to know with absolute certainty, with no shadow of doubt in your minds at all, this then, is the same energy and strength of mind that you must put to dealing with things where you are asking for a miracle to occur.

You must be able to see, and develop that spiritual eye so that in the seeing, you change the condition in your minds. Change it from that decayed disease to the perfect stamp of body, and perfect way, that cures and pushes away disease itself.

It is a GROWING CERTAINTY that we want you to have. A growing certainty, without a doubt that God is able to do this when you are healing a condition of the body - to lay your hands upon them and know that you are taking away that condition - taking it away. In the Power that God possesses, is the ability to dematerialise anything within the body that is a disease, or a form of disease. Like cancer, even AIDS, There is nothing that cannot be taken away by that energy of God.

This is the belief that you must have, and it must be so strong that no doubts whatever can come into your minds and suggest other things. Things like 'It can be done, but I am not good enough'. That is your weakness straight away. It will not happen because you don't believe it, It can be done, because God is doing it. Not me, and it matters little what I can do.

These are the gifts of the spirit that you are growing towards and becoming aware of. The more you strive to achieve one of these gifts, the nearer you become to the realisation of all that I have been saying, Where all things are possible. ALL THINGS ARE POSSIBLE.

So day by day, as you go about your lives, there are those tests that are placed in your way, where you may use your understanding, and use the degree of the gift to its fullness, or fail, according to your mind, according to your light of spirit.

You must take greater notice of what you think, what you say, and how you act, FOR THIS IS NOT A JOKE, that we are telling you. It is extremely difficult to put into words, but it is never, ever a joke. It is the fulfillment that you seek for in coming not only close to God, but knowing who you are, and performing the works of God, that they may be performed through you by the grace of His holy spirit.

We start then, by looking at ourselves. We challenge ourselves. We see what we have done during the course of the day. What we have said during the course of the day. Have we acted in that spiritual manner that God expects of us? Or have we said and done things to suit our own satisfaction?

Much of the time you will not know. Some of the time you will be sure. The things you do not know, you will come to know, through the constant challenge of life. Each time, you will see it more clearly, and understand it in a more perfect-way. So that you may say to yourselves "Yes, I did that for the right reasons".

Little by little, you will find that the understanding of these things is more clear within you. You will be able to speak about them in a way which you could never do before, because they are in your minds, and they have found words, and it has brought you a little closer to the other side of that gulf which you are trying to span.

So my children, I want you to think about those things, for each day that goes by does not return, and each opportunity that is lost, is gone for ever and cannot be relived. You are the creators of your own lives, and the energies and the forces that you use are of your own choosing, out of your free will. So choose wisely then, consider well what energy you will apply. Will it be one of a creative nature, or will it be one of a destructive nature? These are the things that you must segregate and use.

We all know which ones we SHOULD use, and what is best to do, but very often we find ourselves doing the reverse thing. Not carrying out the will of God, but carrying out our own wills. That is not generating anything of any real value within you.

Have you any questions you would like to ask? For I know how difficult it was for me to explain it, and if there are things that you don't understand, I perhaps can help you with them now.

Q: Are you saying that because conditions were not as course years ago as they are now, that we are all less spiritual today?

Hafed: No, I am not saying that at all. I am saying that although your conditions are more difficult, more course, that is not the reason why you have this obstacle of trying to find how to become more spiritual. They were no more spiritual in those days than you are now.

Q: I don't understand what the obstacle is now, compared to then.

Hafed: The obstacle is the same. They never were any different.

Q: I found difficulty in linking it to what was said last week. We were talking about it being different in those days.

Hafed: Only different in as much as in those days, the earth wasn't polluted. The minds of men were not polluted, and this is the difference that lies between the two worlds. Of course, they were to this end more, I do not want to use the word ignorant, for that is wrong, but they were more simple, more simplistic, if you like. They did not have the advancements of science that you have today, but then they did not have the pollution that you have today either. All that advancement has inclined to change the thinking of man, and the beliefs that man has regarding God and life after death. Does that suffice as an answer to you?

Q: Yes. I think I was mixing it up with the talk on healing, about why it is difficult today to the way it was then.

Hafed: Are you referring to the miracles that happened years ago?

A: Yes.

Hafed: That is right. You see, if you look at those miracles that happened, you must ask yourself "Who did they happen through?" Do you understand me? They were God's servants,

weren't they? They were prophets, holy men. And of course there was the Lord Himself, who was the greatest healer that the world has ever known.
Q: Are we too polluted now, to have people that spiritual?
Hafed: No, you are not. You are indeed, all growing towards that end. But, it is what you must learn. It cannot be given to you. It just doesn't happen like that. It is what is in you, what type of person you are. How much light you have within you. How much love there is in you. These are the things that matter.
Q: If we had prophets today that they had in those days, perhaps that would turn the world around?
Hafed: It never did so! Did it? It never did so in their day, and I have no doubt that it won't in this day. If the Lord Jesus was to appear on the streets of London today, preaching and healing, He would come to the same end. They would be trying to put Him in a mad house. Or those who saw Him as a friend, would try and push Him towards the kind of life that they had, where greed and position and money were concerned. They would surely try to put an end to Him. I don't think they would be any the more prepared to stay and listen and learn and change. I think it would be the same.
Q: Are there people walking the earth today who have reached that perfect state?
Hafed: The sons of God? Yes there are those on earth, but they do not advertise the fact, for they have other things to do, and it is not yet the will of God to use them in that way.
Q: They are biding their time?
Hafed: Biding their time is perhaps wrong, for they are doing the work that they are here to do. A work that man cannot understand, by dispersing bands of evil and bringing light to those places that are caught up in darkness through the power of evil, and except that they should do this, then little by little that evil would grow and the darkness would grow, and spread across the entire world that you live in. It would envelope every mind and every heart, and you would all become as violent and sick as the next man. Indeed, it would put an end to

free will, for there would be no spiritual progression, and that is what free will is really there for. So that you may progress. You understand me?

Q: Yes. You have made it very clear.

Hafed: Does anyone else have a question?

Q: It seems to me, that the greatest thing to grasp is the power of love. We must love at all times.

Hafed: That is right. But it is not just a question of knowing that love exists, it is a question of using it, and becoming part of it. In that way, because love is an energy for good, it is a creative energy - then all things around around you will be created in the same mould of love, and bring peace and joy not only to you, but to those who link with you. It is a God power, and if you grasp that, and put it to use, you are a long way indeed towards the fulfillment of becoming the son of God.

Any other questions? Then I will take my leave of you.

THE GOLDEN AGE

Good afternoon, God bless you my children. It is very pleasant to come together again and sit in this atmosphere of peace and love, and to see so many of you striving to understand what God is and who you are.

Since you have become more acquainted with your God, I suppose there are those moments in your lives when you find it difficult to keep your feet upon the pathway, that He has asked for you to do. Difficult in the sense of being able to uphold and follow His laws, and maybe this breaking of those laws at times will only be small, but make you feel a little sad, hurt even.

It is all to be expected, there is no shame in not being able to uphold those spiritual laws in your lives, for the more you strive the better you are able to pursue the way that is set before you, and the easier it becomes to meet the challenge that comes to you from your lower, weaker self.

There is as I have said, no shame attached to this. The shame only comes if you do not try to overcome it. For the more that you gather to yourselves of truth and love, the greater shall be your strength to meet it each time that it appears.

These things are with you for that very purpose. To teach you and to strengthen you, that you may come face to face with that reflection of the truth in you, and that you may decide once and for all, which way you are going to travel, whether it is with the wind, or whether it is against it. For the branches bend when the wind comes, else they will snap. And so it is with you, my children. You too must bend with the wind, else you will snap.

In you is growing a flower of faith, and that flower is very delicate. The storms of life that blow against it can be very damaging if you do not take care. We have said to you at times, that all these spiritual virtues that you are striving to raise up within you, are not only going to change you, but will add to you the fabric of the spirit which will garb you in a new awareness of life.

In your scriptures it is written, 'I have cast you all in the same mould, that mould is in my likeness'. So God then, has made each and every one of us, and fashioned us, in His likeness, but not in the likeness of physical flesh and bone, but fashioned us in the spirit that He is.

Jesus speaking to the woman at the well said, "There comes a time when your Father and my Father no longer wishes for man to pray to Him in temples made with hands, but to pray to Him in spirit and in truth. For your heavenly Father is spirit".

When you sit here and look around the group, you recognise each other by your faces, and by the names that have been given to you. But how do you recognise God? How do you see yourselves? There is no comparison, you know, between the reflection of yourself in a mirror, and the real you.

Let me offer an example so that you can begin to see something of what I mean. If you hold in the palm of your hand the seed of a flower, and look at it - such a tiny mite of a thing, it is almost impossible to realise that from that tiny speck, a flower will grow, bearing the majesty of God in all its beauty, and will be designed in a special way that cannot in any way be seen or imagined by looking at that tiny seed.

Where does that power come from? Where is the life that is in it? It is almost by magic that these things happen. The end product is a beautiful thing that has been raised up from Mother Earth by the power and grace of God,

So then, the thing that you see is not the thing it is going to be, and that is like you, who sits here now. What you see now is not the thing that is going to be. You are like the seed that you have in your hands. None of you can in any way realise what is going to transform from you having lived here in this world.

You cannot imagine what love is going to transform you into, and all those other spiritual qualities, when they raise you up to your full and beautiful potential.

Had you never ever seen a flower before in your lives, and somebody had placed that seed in your hand and tried to tell you what was going to become of it, such a thing could never have entered into your mind. Even if you allowed your imagination to run wild, you could never have guessed, because it was light years away from your mode of thinking. Your ability to think. You could never have captured the truth about that tiny seed.

If then you could not see or imagine what was to evolve from that seed, because it was beyond the reach of your mind, how then are you going to see what is to become of YOU? Is that not also light years away from your thinking?

If all this is true, what then of God? How do you measure, by the yard or foot of your mind, the substance of God that has created all these things? There is no way. No way that man, no matter how clever, could ever begin to have those thoughts and ideas fashioned in his mind, as to what is to transform from you, and what God has already transformed into, It is beyond you. You could not begin to guess.

The scientist, with all his knowledge and skills at his finger tips, when it comes to unravelling the mysteries of life, and the power that is locked up in a tiny seed, is totally lost. For there is no way, no way at all, that he could make a tiny seed such as this. Least of all put within it the power, that it will transform itself into a beautiful flower.

I tell you these things because I want to try to capture the image of those words, and what they are trying to paint for you. I realise of course, how difficult it is to capture the full image of what is there, in its entirety, in its understanding, but hopefully I have given you some kind of yardstick by which to measure yourself and what is to be, and of course, of God, which is far beyond the ability of your mind.

All these things are there as a pointer for man, to point him in the right direction. That he may see and say to himself, "I accept all these things, and never give thought to how they came into being, or why. Nor have I considered the greater and wiser power that is in existence, which has created and designed all these things. That in itself is evidence of God, that cannot in any way, shape or form, be disputed, and yet it is never ever noticed.

In many ways, nature teaches us a number of things. It reveals not only the nature of God that is within them, but reveals to us how we should be, and how we are going to change, transformed in a way that you cannot see, but is none-the-less changing. This is why I spoke to you in the beginning, about facing up to the frailties within you.

All of you do not have the same frailties. You have different ones which you must strive to overcome. Do not feed them by giving them pride of place in your lives, but deny them all the strength and energy that you can, realising that you will not win every time, for the weaker man always falls to the stronger. But we are not talking about physical strength, so that law can be reversed. We are speaking of the spiritual strength, and that law can win for you every time.

My children, even as blessed as you are with many of God's truths, you are blind to the things around you. You have learned to see them in a different way from what they really are. You miss the point that they are trying to reveal to you.

You are looking for contentment and happiness, and yet keep running down the wrong pathway - the one that leads only to your misery. Time and time again, you run down that road, only to come to grief, until you learn.

"Has this not happened before? Have I not been down this road before, and what was at the bottom? Did I gain anything that I really wanted? Or did I lose sight of the things that were precious to me?"

It has never been God's will that His children should live in misery, poverty and disease. It is always mans' will through following the wrong laws, of greed, of jealousy and hatred, that has set these things in motion.

It is written in the scriptures, that the meek will inherit the earth. When you sit and think about it, it looks impossible, for where are the meek now? How long is this going to take - for ever? It is greatly misunderstood, for while the earth is in its present condition, the meek can never inherit it. The earth can never be as God wants it to be.

But, you know, those words were not said for nothing. For the mystery of them is like the flower and the seed. It is hidden from your eyes, hidden from your mind.

It is also written, that in the time of Aquarius, the children of light shall be born. If you link the two together, we are speaking about the same thing. We are speaking about the meek who will inherit the earth.

I have said to you, that the children of light are not babies who are waiting to be born, but those already living. Many have through the wisdom and truth of God captured that meekness, captured that childlike manner once again, as they try to see and understand with their mind's eye, for out of the womb of misery, will be born the children of light, will be born the meek.

If you have listened intently to some of the talks that I have given you in the past, you will recall I spoke about the change that is to come into the world. I spoke to you first about the great upheaval that must take place, then told you that out of this upheaval would come forth the meek. For those who have seen wars, great terror and fear, afterwards ARE meek.

I know that a lot of you are too young to have been through the last world war, but I am certain that if you have heard from others who have, that during that time there was a great brotherhood among the nations that were at war with Germany. There was a friendship that grew up between neighbours and those whom they did not know, that is not abroad today. For they were all willing to help each other. It was because of the calamity and the great fear that was there in those war days with the bombing. Out of that evil they learned to reach into themselves, and found a kind of comfort in that companionship with each other. A kind of meekness,

That is what creates it, and shows it to man, when he runs amok with his instruments of destruction. Tearing down peoples homes and lives, and bringing them to their knees in fear. When they are able to raise their heads again, it is as one who is humble and thankful to God for bringing them through the night safely.

I have spoken of a time that is to be. That is greater in fear and destruction than ever before. Those who survive shall be the meek.

It has been said that the Lord Jesus will return again, and so it shall be. And in that time, when that has happened, shall there grow a great bond between all men. There will be a great love enter their hearts, and a great cry to their God for salvation. The time will be as in the very beginning of time, when man lived in a state of being far removed from what you know now. That time when the wise ones called it 'The Golden Age'.

There will be a thousand years of peace so it is written. This is the time which I speak of, and this is the time which is to be completely the reverse of the world that you know now.

For in that time, the power that is locked up in a tiny seed of the flower and the trees, shall be let loose, and the earth will be filled with life again. Man will be raised up as friend and neighbour, and will then, in that time, know why they must walk according to the laws of God and not according to their own wants, desires, and greed, which has brought the world to a near catastrophe of total destruction.

In that time shall they know these things, and thank their God that they have been saved from them. For except that it be for God, then no flesh could live on earth.

There will be a new kingdom that will be raised up. There will be a new order of life, a new law which will stand fast in the hearts of man, and in the mind of man. For the trees shall bear their fruit, and man shall no longer sup at the table with meat, but will eat the fruit of the earth. The birds of the air will truly be free, and fear nothing. For no fear shall be in the hearts of all life in that time.

This is the time when the lion shall lay down with the lamb, and there shall be no anger between them. Man shall not work for gain, for treasure. Neither shall there be one above the other, telling him what to do and where to go.

There shall be no government, only the ruler in your heart which will be God. He shall come and dwell with His children, in their midst. That which they work for, shall be each other and not for themselves or anyone else, and the kingdom that they build shall be blessed with peace. There shall be no more of the anguish that exists between man. No more shall there be the rape of children, and the taking of life, for all that will no longer exist.

Neither shall any one man say, "This house is mine. I own it". Or, "I will fence this field and no man shall enter, because it is my land". All men will know that everything belongs to all. There is no one who owns more than another. But God has given it to all.

Neither shall man have to strive for food, neither shall he have contaminated land or water, for all will be sweet and life giving.

It will be a totally different world. A world where neither the heat of summer will cause you discomfort, nor the harshness of the winter will give you pain. Where disease will be banished, and it shall not be with you again.

All that is necessary for that better life shall be yours. You will then know what freedom really is. For you will not be tied in one place, and confined in one place, neither shall your mind be inhibited from reaching out and understanding and grasping greater truths than you have ever known before.

When man takes a woman to wife, it truly will be for life. Their love will be for always. Their children shall be their blessing, and they shall raise them in the sight of their God according to how God had instructed.

There shall be no more death as you know it. For when death comes to you now, your body is buried and those who loved you are then separated from you, for your spirit can no longer be seen. But in that life and time, because of the spiritual light that will emanate, the physical body as you now know it will take on a different softness, a different texture. One that is more in keeping with the spirit body. One shall not die in the sense that I have explained, but through their progression shall travel on to other parts of God's kingdom. To that higher realm that they have reached and found.

But they will not leave behind them loved ones who will yearn for them, and have tears for them, and they shall see them no more. For they will be able to be with them at any time, and they will not be separated by the fact that the spirit is unseen, but they will be able to see each other, and caress each other, as always. Therefore death as you know it, shall no longer be possible,

Man will progress from this earth, and simply go on to a higher realm, returning whenever he wishes to see those he has left, until they, when their turn comes, will also journey on to where he or she is at that moment, in that different sphere of life.

So my children, I have tried to paint a picture the best I can, of a way of life that is perhaps unbelievable to you, and I cannot in any way say that if you don't believe it I would be troubled in mind. I can only say that some of you here in this room will witness that new world. Others of you will not. So time itself will reveal the truth to you, and realising in yourself that there must be a time to come when all of these things which are promised must come right.

God bless you. Farewell, farewell.

GOLDEN SILENCE

Good afternoon and God bless you my children.

They say that the golden silence is one to search for. Others say that silence is golden. Either way, it holds a great deal, and if man should teach himself such things, it would indeed be a golden life that he would have.

Well I know that last week we spoke to you of the Golden Age, and it is not my intention to stay with you for very long this afternoon, but I want to say a few words, and if by saying them I am able to show you the errors of man, you will at least have learned something.

It is only when man allows his own thoughts and feelings to rise to the forefront, that they overcome and transgress the law of God. For man will insist on trying to become the authority, rather than the child who sits and listens. Not always is it possible for you to totally understand the word of God as it is given to you. Very often, you misinterpret the ways that God intended you to follow.

If you look in your scriptures, you will discover that there are three great religions, although I do not like the word religion, for it does not really apply itself to the truth of God.

None-the-less, there are three that man follows, religions that God has given to him.

The first, as well you know, was the Jewish faith, born out of Abraham. To this day they still follow much of what was written. Then of course, there was the Christian religion, which seemed to be a follow-on to the religion of the Jews. Then there was also Islam, a follow-on from Christianity.

If you were to look into all those religions, you would find the same law of life and living was applied to all of them. The same truths are there to be seen clearly, and in each case it was God's intention that man should live with man, in peace. that there should be this great bond between them.

We find that out of the Jewish faith was born the son of God, who, through His teachings the Gentiles created the Christian religion. Again, out of Mohammed came Islam. If you look, it comes back into one circle, for Islam has within its teachings been told by God, through Mohammed, that the Jewish faith, and also the Christian faith, ARE ALL ONE FAITH. That Jesus was born out of Mary who was a virgin, and He indeed is the Son of God, and that each of them should be treated as they would their own.

So God intended that each of those three religions should become as one, and should inherit the same truth and the same way of living. But over the course of time you can see how those very religions have been segregated. How in Islam, they are at war with both the Jewish nation, and also with the Gentiles. You can see in the Jewish faith how they too are at war with Islam, and will not have anything to do with Jesus as the Son of God. They will not accept Him.

And so you have left to you the faith that is the Christian, which, as I have already said, is also in effect, at war with Islam and the Jewish faiths. So all of them have completely separated from each other. All of this is because those in that faith - which ever faith it was - did not listen to the words that were given to them by their prophets and teachers. Had they done so, there could be no separation, neither could they be one at war with the other.

It is only the hatred of man and the ignorance of man prevailing over religion, rather than God, and it is these that have injected their own ideas, their own views, and their own interpretations into the prophets words, and caused them to be very damning to each of the others religions that they are supposed to support.

When you consider this, you will realise that had man listened to the words of God, the word that He gave them, the situation that exists within the Middle East today, affecting all other countries that are either Christian or of the Jewish faiths, or Islamic, is in effect the very situation that God had hoped to avoid when He first gave them those words of truth to lead them by.

There could never have been the suffering that has gone on in the Middle East, either between the Jewish nation and the Arab world, or even the suffering that has gone on within the Arab world itself against each other. Neither would there have been this hatred that exists between one nation and the other, that uphold these religions.

So you begin to understand how it is that man, through not listening to the given word, created conditions that he cannot see and understand the end product of. Years ago, when all these things began to fall apart, those in that time could not see where it would all lead them in terms of the present-day conditions. No more than the present day conditions can be seen by those who are yet to come. Or what kind of world they are creating out of the noise that they are making.

Because man is devious, and not trustworthy or faithful, there is no saying that because he makes a pact with this country or that country, that such pacts will be kept. That is just something that is suitable to those and their cause at that moment of time, but which may give great aggravation to those in the days to come.

So, it would seem to me, that had they kept silent, and not allowed all this aggravation and hatred to build up within them - kept their peace and their silence and followed the word of God that was given to them by instruction through the prophets of old, they would have allowed the laws of God to have worked out all their problems, and there would have been none doing battle with another, for how could there be when you follow the same God?

Because they let go of those things, and turned to their own devices to satisfy their own greed, so the pain and suffering begins. Many thousands, yea even millions, suffer a great torment because of it all.

How do you think God feels right now when they have taken His word and twisted it out of all proportion. When they have rejected all His laws of love and peace? What else is He able to do?

It seems to me that man is not only determined to destroy all that he believes in and all the good that was there, but also to destroy himself.

We continue in prayer, that God's will may be done with them, for the good of every nation on earth.

With that I will leave you, and say no more. Good afternoon, and God bless you all.

THE GIFT OF PEACE

I greet you beloved, in the name of love, and in the name of Him whom I call Lord and Master. Peace be with you.

Always on this day, we find great joy in being able to come among you in this sweet way. Feeling the love and also the excitement that comes from you, stimulates us and draws us ever closer to you. For we come with the Master's love and the Master's blessing for you all, and realising that Christmas draws ever nearer, we would try to bring a few words that will enlighten you as to the coming of Jesus, and all that He endeavoured to fulfill in His life.

We would like to set this present day and time against that of yesteryear. So that we may be able to fix in our minds the two pictures - that which man holds true today, and that which is true of yesteryear.

My children, I want you, if you will, to imagine a certain night, many years ago, when the very air itself was filled with a kind of stillness, that set the heart aflame with expectations.

I want you to see a bright star, as it hung there in the sky over a stable. A very unimportant place, where you would think to yourself 'No king could ever be born there', and yet, with this wondrous night was born a child, the child Jesus. He who it had been promised for many hundreds of years, was to come. Emmanuel.

That night was not without merriment, joy, and peace. For these were the gifts of the spirit given to man who was in that location at the time. A great joy filled the hearts of all, both rich and poor, both mighty and lowly. There were the angels who gathered around the shepherds on the hillside, and through this stillness of the night that seemed to crackle with excitement, sung those words, 'Peace on earth and goodwill towards all men'.

All of this, my children, I want you to see as being the gift given to man by God, and I want you to see how those gifts were priceless. Could not be bought anywhere in your world, regardless of how much money was paid, or offered. They were priceless.

For they stilled the angry mind, and the sad and suffering hearts, and brought to them a way of life that was so much more perfect than they had. A perfection in joy and peace. 'Peace on earth, goodwill towards all men'.

Over the course of time, down to your present age, the birthright of Jesus seems to have been stolen by this man Father Christmas, and in its place, in place of those spiritual gifts, that if man would still seek for, would find, have been put the treasures that man himself looks for, and desires. All of which are of an earthly nature, and pamper his vanity.

We have heard, in the prayer, (reference to a prayer said by one of the group members before Hafed had commenced speaking), regarding the children of earth and how there will be some sad faces this Christmas. My brethren, they will not be so sad as maybe you imagine. We have heard that perhaps miracles will occur, and I have no doubts that that will happen, but not in the way that you suppose. For God has no presents for man of an earthly nature, for to give him these would rob him of the finer gifts that will enhance his spirituality.

We, on the other hand, have no tears for those who are poor and perhaps will be without, but sadness we have for those who will have been given far too much. Hence their values will be out of proportion to the reality of what Christ Jesus came to show - those values of the spirit and of the soul, not to add to the greed of man, but to add to the goodwill towards all men, by that peace, forgiveness and love in that merriment that took place all that time ago, took place in the hearts and minds of men who linked with those heavenly beings, filled with the presence of Christ.

In this day and time, Father Christmas leaves upon your trees nothing that can be compared with that. For in mans' seeking for merriment, it very often leads him to tears. It leads him to that time and place where his joy is overtaken by his drinking, and his actions lead to marriage breakdowns, and little children with heartaches because of it all.

If you look, you can see the two different values. One which comes from your God and is of Heaven, and the other which is born out of the carnal thoughts and desires of man, none of which provide for his true happiness.

Man seeks those kinds of pleasure that will cause pain, out of his boredom, because he has need of somewhere to go, something to do. But those very things which he seeks to give him release from boredom, in reality cause it. Create that depression that comes after that kind of excitement.

So do not be partakers of that kind of bread, my children.

For while it is on your tongue it may taste well, but when it is in your stomach you will revolt against it, and it will cause all kinds of pain.

Look towards that which was heard and felt on the rejoicing of the first Christmas night, when the young Saviour was born among us. What He was to tell us, and fill us with. Words of great price, bread from heaven.

Many of you may think that the spirit world itself is the kingdom of heaven, but it is not. Many places in that same world are far from being near to heaven, but are filled with the shame and bitterness and darkness of man through the works that he has created in his life. In that place there is no law, and there is no order of thing. Man is an individual going from place to place in his wanderings.

The approach roads to God are those in the spheres that lie BEYOND the spirit world and lead to that city whose very foundation, whose maker and builder is God. This is where we are leading you when we give you words which are filled with light and purpose, and destine you to walk that road which will be one of great joy in the end.

You can only fool yourselves my children, you cannot fool God if you try still to hide behind the real cloak that you wear, and yet try to deceive others that you wear something brighter. The deceit is for yourselves, and no one else.

I suppose it has never crossed your minds to ask how you stand on the ladder of progression. Can any of you here tell me this?

A: Yes. At the bottom.

Hafed: Can any of you tell me then, out of all that I have said to you over the course of the months that you have been coming here, how can you judge how far up the ladder you have come?

A: By listening to you.

Hafed: Yes, but there is another way.

A: By the values that you hold.

Hafed: Yes, but there is yet another way, a more certain way, and only you can know it. No one else, only you.

A: How we cope with our lives.
A: I think it is the feeling of peace perhaps. Inner peace?
A: Through the feeling of love.
A: I think it is the faith within yourself, when you look at how you were before, and how you are now.
Hafed: Yes, yes, that is a true reflection in many ways. But there is one more certain way that cannot in any way be hidden from you. Can be hidden from others, but can never be hidden from you, and that, my children, if you wish to know, I will tell you.

When you have dealings in your world with various other people, perhaps there are times when things go wrong for you. Maybe someone will say something out of place. If you can ignore that, and there is no resentment in you, no desire to answer back or retaliate, then you can say that you have passed that stage in your progression where it will affect you. You are beyond that.

But look for the time when suddenly, something may happen, and though you may not speak what your inner feelings are telling you, you feel hurt and bitter. Then when you experience that feeling of resentment, know that that is the limit of your progression. That you have not gone beyond that point. Do you understand me? That is a more direct way of knowing. A way that you yourselves can see and understand.

Also realise this, that as long as you go along that road, you will begin to sense and feel the spiritual truths that are born in you. You will begin to see and understand those truths in far greater detail then you do now. And yet it does not mean to say that that truth is part of you, just because you can see it. Just because you can understand it. Just because you want that truth to be part of you. It must be that you live that truth, and that the truth is you. It has to become part of the garb that you wear, is woven into that garb.

And so my children, you begin to understand that what you are, you remain. Even though you listen to me, and hear the truths that I have told you, and you are striving to live according to them, that is something that you must always do, even though there are those times when it reflects in you a kind of feeling that is not bitterness or hatred, but a little resentment, because the root of that real truth is not there.

So, you cannot be greater than what you are, spiritually. The spiritual essence of your progression has reached a set point. You cannot travel beyond it, because you do not have that ability within you, but always are striving to go that step further. Knowing inwardly, that it is wrong to resent that kind of thing, regardless of how small or how great it may be, it is wrong. Thus you are in effect, not living according to the laws of God. Neither are you finding within yourselves that great peace towards all men.

So, this is the stage of progression that you are at. And you are all at different levels of that progression. And you, and only you know how far it goes. How deep it is within you, where you can reject it. No one can change you, you can only change yourselves by seeing the reality of truth in the words that are given to you, and thus striving to overcome that darkness within you, to make it into light.

This is why, when you pass into the world of spirit, you have that approach road. For that approach road is your opportunity to develop your soul in that greater spiritual light and fulfillment of understanding according to what God has placed in you. Little by little you travel along that road, back to that city that has foundation, whose maker and builder is God, and which - it is written - is Heaven.

So you see, my children, Christmas is not always what you think, and not always what you see. For there are many people in your world who fear Christmas. Fear it because of what it will bring, because there are those in the family who cannot behave themselves, who have no control over their lives and cannot set themselves free from that obsession, be it women, be it money, be it drink, drugs, or any of those things which belong to the weaker man. That is their fear.

It is not just where husband and wife are concerned. In your world now, it is where their children are concerned, for they indeed grow up in very strange times. Times that offer them the destroyer of their souls, their hearts and their minds, because the spiritual values have never been indoctrinated in them from childhood.

They have never ever been brought before their God, and set that standard of being in motion in their lives. Their mothers and fathers react to each other in front of their children, with words which are upsetting enough, but the children listen, and they think it all part of life, and they use these words which are foul in every sense.

They are allowed to watch all kinds of violent and sexual scenes which are all on the perimeter of hell, make no mistake about that. They are not accord to the law of God. When you think about it, truly think about it, you must be able to see how those things bring only corruption, and destroy any chance that you may have of happiness. Because they are motivated by the forces of evil, not the forces of good. Not what Jesus brought and showed man.

It is our hope that you may go forward and teach man of these things in the times to come. Not all of you, but there are hopes for most. But if you cannot do these things for yourselves, if you cannot be who you say you are, then there is no hope that you will begin to show these truths to others. For you will be known for your fruits, and if your fruits are evil, then so will you be. Corrupt. If your sweets are sweet and good, then so will you be - spiritually alight with promise.

We who congregate here, from our side of life - from the realms of light, wish to impart to you this Christmas, a gift of the spirit. That same gift that was given to me and many others in that time when the Lord Jesus was born. For I was privileged to be present on that occasion, and that gift you will not purchase anywhere in this world. For it is beyond price. It is the gift of peace. So settle it in your hearts, and go with that great joy and those good tidings of peace on earth and goodwill towards all men.

Such things as these can never come, until man has them in his heart. We give them to you this Christmas, as your spiritual gift. It is for you to take, or to leave, as you see fit. But remember, you will find no greater gift this Christmas than the one that we have given you. For it is the bread of life, and comes from the Lord's table. If you receive it, it can establish itself in your hearts for all time, and bring to you the magic of God. THE MAGIC OF GOD is something which you have all yet to experience, but when you do, my children, you will understand why, on our side of life, there is nothing like the boredom that you experience in your lives.

So, with these words, my children, I will leave you until another time, and hope that you have been able to drink the elixir of life that we have given you. May it fill your being with its joy.

Good afternoon. Farewell, farewell.

THE CHURCH OF SALVATION

Peace be with you my children, and God bless you.

Always it is a joy to come among you, especially to those with like minds, and this particular day gives even greater joy to us who travel back through time to be here with you.

You may not understand that word time, and yet in effect, that is what we do. For once there was a time when I lived in the past, and you were yet to come, in the future. In a time too, when there was great rejoicing, and certainly great rejoicing in my heart, because I was one of the privileged bearers of the gifts that were to be delivered to that young child, so long ago.

But then, like all men, I too had to travel on, and hope that in some way I had made a mark upon this world. And my work is still there, even to this day, for when my Master was crucified, I travelled back to my own land, and began the first

Christian church ever to be built. There it still stands even now, in my country which was Persia.

So now I come back to you from the past to speak to you in the present, but a time will come when you too will make that change called death, and hope to leave your mark also. A mark that will stand good for as many a year as the one that I was fortunate enough to make. For I have given to you, my children, all the good blessings that were given to me by Him who I call Lord and Master. There are none to whom I have not given, and yet greater is still to come, for the blessings of the Lord Himself are yet to come.

So, at this festive time, I bring to you that double indemnity of the Holy Spirit - the Christmas Spirit, that I give to each one as their present for this year, that they may carry that light within their hearts and minds, and embrace all others within that light.

How joyful I am, when I look round and see how you, my children, have embraced all the knowledge of wisdom that we have given, and how your love has grown, your understanding has grown, and how that feeling of goodwill survives here in this sanctuary, among you. And so it is our hope that that goodwill may grow even brighter as time does pass, for it has not been called God's circle for nothing. There is a great reason for that. A reason that has yet to be revealed.

As once I built the first Christian church, you who are here, are to do exactly as I did, but with a greater effect. For in this time, you are to lighten up that truth in the minds of all those who will come and participate. On the horizon there is also a meeting place, where you all will take part, and have your work. A church of salvation, a church of great truth, a church that preaches only the Christ truth, and has the good Shepherd as its Teacher.

In the year that is soon to open for us, you are then going to be about your Father's business. For here you will come, week after week, and you will have your spiritual gifts unravelled. Slowly at first, but then they will accelerate as the time is right.

Some of you will go faster along that road than others. Do not worry, do not fear, for your time is also to come, for in all minds there must be the same light that burns, that faith - the oil of faith, must burn within your minds. That great sword of truth must be carried by all. Those words of wisdom that strike dumb those who are the avenging angels of deceit and evil.

For many will come, looking to you for that greater light, for peace, because they are filled with despair and can find no comfort in the world at large. But it will be in your hands, my children. It will be your gift to give man.

Of course it will demand more time from you, for if we are to open and build this church, then it is to be with you as the very foundation, as the nucleus, of all that is good within it. For a church or a building of any kind is not made of bricks and mortar alone, for the strength of that church must be in your love and your faith to God, your love to your fellow man, your faith in your God, that you know that with Him, all things are possible.

Never lose sight of that, my children, for so often you do. With God all things are possible. For God can indeed work miracles in His own way, and still does, and you will be witness to those very miracles to be worked.

I want you to mark this first Christmas for we are growing, my children, not only in our love for each other, but also in power and in strength. As time passes, and each one of you is raised up in the Christ spirit, and has those spiritual morals engraved in your hearts, then so will that power grow even greater, and many wonderful things will happen among you, and you will see, and you will know, that that means the fulfillment of my words has come true.

It is all down to you. Keep faith with me, and we will surely keep faith with you. The greater light is still to come, and the greater joy is still to be revealed. No greater shall that joy be than when you yourselves feel the presence of that Christ spirit raised up within you, and those ministering angels from the realms of light gather about you, and you feel the warmth that you belong to the family of God, and belong to no other.

As I sit here now, and see the many bright souls gathering about you, none brighter than the little children whom this festive season is really for, for they and they alone carry something of that Christ spirit, and here they are gathering about you, some of them known to you and some of them not. Here too, are your mothers and fathers and your grandparents and uncles and aunts, all are here, wearing that garb of light. All here with that festive spirit of goodwill towards men and peace on Earth.

So, as the cup of life is passed round to each of you, in a symbolic way, drink deep of that cup, my children. For the wine that it contains is the very spirit of life, and know what it truly means to be the hand-maiden of God, to be the servant of God. Yes, even as Mary was chosen as one special, so you too can feel that holy presence of God. Holy, holy, holy in His name. Accept none other than He.

I will now leave you, for there are others who love you and wish to draw near to you, to impart some Christmas greetings of their own.

Farewell, farewell.

MANIPULATING THE POWER OF GOD

Good afternoon and God bless you, my children. Peace be with each and every one of you.

It has become a great joy to me on these occasions, when my children are gathered together in the sanctuary of God. Not always can I say that I have such pleasing thoughts wherever I go, for there are those places that I go to where it does not please me at all. But this is one of the better tasks that are given to me to perform.

Always I long for you to hear my words, not just to know what they mean, but to totally understand that in them somewhere is the very seed of life that you are looking for. For the answers to all your questions are there, locked away in all those many teachings that I have given to you in the past. In each word there is a power that is almost magic, for it offers you guidance. Not guidance in the form of clairvoyance, that tells you of events to come, but a different kind of guidance that tells you how to control the events come.

Perhaps you haven't given that much thought. Perhaps you see those events in front of you as being beyond your control. Something that is going to happen, regardless of what you will do. But then, if that were so, then your free will would count for nought.

No, what we try to do, is to control the events for you, because we know that you cannot control them yourselves at this time in life. Meaning to say that our work on your behalf on this side of life, is to build for you a road that is leading you to the events of the future that will be pleasing for you, and satisfying not always in an earthly way, but certainly in a spiritual way.

But you know, my children, there comes a time when you cannot go any further, unless you take the materials that are there in those words and begin to build your future for yourselves, and control the events that are there for you. You may say to me, "But my life is bound up in so many different ways with the events of governments and powers that be, and people that are not very reliable. How then, can I plan events?"

You can, to this end. By using the power that we have given to you in the words of the teachings. But it takes a great deal for you to read them, and become fully mindful of what lies within every word, and what lies behind every word, and to put it into practice so that the power of those words become established in you.

For example, if I may use your lives in the material sense

to say to you, that if you desire to go swimming, you do so either by going to a seaside resort, or to your swimming baths. You do not go to a supermarket. Neither do you go to the woods. For you know that neither of those places can fulfill your desire. So in that sense then, you are aware of where you must go to accomplish your own personal desires. that is using the commonsense that has been instilled in you, over the course of years.

But there is another insight which is not of a spiritual nature, for if you sit and think about what you want out of life, the answer, in a broad sense, is happiness. Now, to accomplish those things, you do not go about making enemies with your neighbours. You do not go about taking drugs, or being violent to strangers on the street. You do not go about holding up banks, or knocking down old ladies for their pensions.

You must realise that none of those things can bring to you the happiness and love that you need in your lives. To do those things would be like trying to swim in a field or in a supermarket. You could not accomplish it. So that same thing applies there.

If you then, want that peace, happiness and love, then you must see to it that your approach to other people is with that same attitude of mind as you would wish them to have for you. You must not be full of hypocritical words, by believing one thing and doing another. You must not allow yourselves to be bitter and full of swear words because somebody has upset you. For as soon as you do that, you depart from the pathway that you say you want to follow.

Now, we have over the course of these past months placed a great emphasis upon spiritual virtues that we want to see grow up within you. If you would recall the very first time we came, we said to you that the first step towards God was honesty. That is one of the virtues, and because you strive to be honest, then you must realise that a change is going to take place within your body, your mind, and within your heart, hence in your life, because those three things govern your life, govern your vision of what you want in that life.

Honesty. It is not an empty word. It is not a sound that fills the air, and then is gone. It is a living force, because it is a spiritual force. It is a virtue of the soul - a virtue of Jesus Christ.

It is of that same seed that has within it a creative energy. Think then about honesty, and what it really means in your life. It means then, for you to become honest. You have to apply it in all your dealings with your friends and neighbours. You have to be honest with them.

It means then, that you must tell the truth, for honesty is a guardian of the truth. Two virtues in one. Honesty and truth. And the creative energy that is within is building within you an insight that you never had before. For it shows you that you can begin to build your life as you want it. You can begin to control the events around you.

Very often people are drawn into the wrong way of thinking and living, because they have no control. They go along with the ideas of others because they are stronger than them, although they have the wrong way of thinking and acting.

God has said to you here, as His ministers, that you shall lead them. Not the other way around, but that you should guide them. He has therefore given to you this new insight of being able to see and create for yourself a pathway, which is leading you into the light. Suddenly we realise, that honesty begets truth, and truth begets light, because it is the truth that will set you free.

So now we have found freedom, we have found light, we have found truth, we have found honesty, because we have taken that one step nearer to God. Isn't that amazing? All those other gifts that God has to offer us, have come from that honesty.

But it is not something you must hold, and think of as a word. You must try to see how that power within is creative, and how you can manipulate it that it may be creative for you.

I wonder how many of you are able to plan what your lives are going to be tomorrow, let alone in six months time, a year's time, ten years time. For the kind of life that we are talking about is outside the realm of materialism. It is the realm of spiritual truth, light and honesty.

When you walk in that light and in that realm, the earthly things cannot touch you, because you are protecting yourself with that power of God. It has become your shield.

Who would then, deal with a person with honesty, unless they had love and could see that not to do so would be harmful to their friend or neighbour, or even a stranger? So love then, must invariably enter into it all. For if you do not love God, how could you take the first step? It is simply that the love is there, but not to the forefront at that time. For love itself is a virtue that brings that power of creation to all the other virtues, and lightens them for you to use them.

They are like tools for you to use. It is a fascinating way of manipulating the gifts of God. If you want to accomplish things with other people, you must not approach them with that bullying way that is so often seen in the world in which you live. For none of that is part of the holy spirit of God, which is being fashioned in you through all those virtues that are coming your way.

You do it with love, with gentleness, with understanding. You do it with honesty. You win the minds of the people with those virtues. Let them see something of the holy spirit at work within you, and their soul gives recognition to that, and sees something there that they should know, and yet don't quite understand.

So then, you are beginning to enlarge the circle of your life, where the ability of control is concerned, because you know how to approach people. You know how to think. You know how to be just, and not to seek for things through using those gifts deceitfully, but always honestly. Always with that noble gesture that is in Christ.

You will find an inner vision that comes from it all, which allows you to see where the dangers along the road are, because you are in harmony with the laws of God, and not with the laws of man which think selfishly, and destructively.

You think with the law of God, and you are able to see where those problems lie.

If they are beyond your capability, then you must lend your thoughts to God. If God does not choose to release you from that there and then, you must be patient and wait until He is ready - until YOU are ready. For maybe it is that there is a lesson there for you to learn. For it is well for you to be told of all these attributes, these spiritual qualities, but have you the ability within yourself to be just as that is? To hold that spiritual value, and be as good as you say you are? That is the difference you see.

You might know what you must be, but if you have not that ability within yourself to use it, then it is because you lack that spiritual progression which only the trials and tribulations which are set before you, can work out, and bring to you.

It was asked last week, whether or not you prayed for each other, by name. Those who were here were asked if they prayed and when was the last time they prayed for a certain member of the circle. It was to their credit that they used that honesty by telling the truth, by saying, "I can't remember", or "I haven't done this".

That is a weakness my children, for prayer to God is bringing you ever closer to that great spirit of creation, of all creation, and bringing alive within you that soul, that child-like soul that you are. And if you say that you love the members of your circle, none of you who know what is going on in the lives of the others, and therefore you must be vigilant for them, by praying for them.

"Father, I ask for your guidance and your love for Terry," or for Mick, Ann, whoever it is that you are praying for. But bring them to God by name. Mention by name in your mind. This brings out both your love for them, and your sincerity. God loves a soul who is humble, for no one can serve God without humility, and you bring that to them in your love for God, your heavenly Father.

Use your minds for the projection of His love. Use your minds to become wise in your choice of words and in your actions towards others. Fill your minds with that light that gives you protection. Protects you from the ignorance that very often will overthrow you. Protects you from the frailties of the human form, which very often creep up on you and overthrow you.

Be strong then in the virtues that God has set before you. He does not expect you to win them immediately, to be able to practice them immediately, but He does expect you to be mindful of them each day, and strive to the best of your ability to bring their creative energies alive within yourselves, that you may control your thinking, control your emotional thoughts, that you may bring not only to yourselves, but to others, happiness. That way you will stay within the light. That way you will be able to see what is coming, for you will be creating those conditions around you that will draw towards you that which is like minded to yourself.

Darkness begets darkness, as evil begets evil. As hatred begets hatred, and violence begets violence. If you know all these things, and have no desire to follow them, then you are truly blessed.

Realise that there is always the struggle that goes on between good and evil. There is a great battle taking place right now, and has been going on for a long time, between good and evil. But I don't want you to focus your minds on such things, I want you to fill your minds with that light that brings peace and happiness, and frees you from that worry and fear that can be there in your minds because you think of evil too much. For when you do that, you give pride of place to it in your life. That is not what we want. Such things are of a destructive nature and bring fear and breed fear within you. That is not the purpose of all those spiritual attributes that you are striving to achieve. Those very things are for your protection against evil. Let God deal with evil, and you deal solely with the injustice and laws of God, and the love that He gives you to share with others, that others might also stand in the same light as you, because you have brought them out of the darkness, into the truth.

So do not abide in those things that are for God to deal with. You are not strong enough to overcome those things. You can however become strong through capturing for yourselves those spiritual virtues of forgiveness, love and humility, understanding, tolerance and honesty. All these things will bring you an abundance of joy and peace. Nothing outside of that will give you happiness or peace, because it is all an illusion.

I hope you will think of my words most carefully, and see how you may put them to work in your lives. Think about them in all the conditions of your lives. In all your dealings with your neighbours and friends. When you see one who you feel is not going the right way, it is not for you to condemn them. It is not for you to send words of bitterness and spite after them. For it is not your life. Worry about your own life, and how you are living that.

You cannot save them. You can only help them by sending your love after them, and your prayers after them. But nothing else.

No my children, the hour grows near for you to learn, to sow the seeds that we have given you in the garden of your minds, that you may grow rich in the food of God. In the food of heaven, in the bread of heaven. The hour grows near, when that love from Him to you must penetrate every fibre of your being, for it is only that which will enhance your spiritual light, and make you a servant of God.

Do not be fooled by the light of the world, and all its promises of riches and fulfillments of dreams. For I tell you that it is a fools illusion, and will bring you nothing and will win nothing, except a great many tears, a great many heartaches, and a fear beyond your understanding at this moment of time,

Such then is the direction that most men in your world are following. Henceforth, you will see what I mean. Many of the devil's servants walk among man, and strive to lead others astray, Be not fearful of them. Do not worry about their doings, but see to it that your minds are focused only on the laws of God, and on the love of God, that you may walk in His light, and manipulate the power that is to be found in those spiritual virtues. For who is to say that you might not win and manipulate them all?, because you can with the fulfillment of what Christ said - "If you had faith so much as a mustard seed, you could tell the mountain, henceforth to be cast into the sea, and it would obey you". For this is the kind of power of which we speak, and what it will transform you into. For such you see, are the Sons and Daughters of God. But this is only the beginning, and is certainly nowhere near the end.

So I will bid you good afternoon one and all. I pray that my words have found a resting place within you, and that my words will not be brought to nought because you failed to listen. Rather, you may see and understand the pricelessness of the gifts that we have brought you.

Good afternoon, and God bless you all.

Clarification of:

JESUS COMING TO BE CRUCIFIED FOR THE SINS OF THE WORLD

Good afternoon and God bless you my children. It is a very pleasant day, is it not?

I thought that this afternoon, we might make a change from our usual procedure where I would come and address you, for surely over the course of time that I have been addressing you, there must have been many questions that have arisen in your minds. I realise that I have not given full attention to them, and therefore I think it would probably be a good thing if we had an open discussion where you might put questions that have formed in your minds over the last few months. So I am going to leave you for five minutes of your time, to sit back and think about what you would like to ask. then you do so, speak up. Do not hold back.

Q: Jesus came to save mankind, to take upon His shoulders the sins of the world, and was crucified, or that is my interpretation. Could you please explain and clarify that for me?

Hafed: This has always been a talking point in the church between those who believe in Christ being the Son of God, and those who believe that Jesus was a mortal man.

Now it is obvious I think, from the works that Jesus did, that He was more than a man. For what man in your world has before or since done such works? There are none. The authority that He took with Him into the world was clear to see in the teachings that He gave, for they were spoken as from One with authority.

Nonetheless, there are still those who cannot see where the truth lies, even though, in His coming, He was the fulfillment of the prophecies that had been made by God's holy men from thousands of years back. His name was declared as One who was to come.

In His coming, His works were so designed as to change the thinking and change the ways of mankind. By doing this, those who followed in that way, were freed from the sins that would have come their way had they gone in another direction. For in man there is always that selfish spark, that greed, that ambition, that is prepared to do all things in order for them to gratify their desires. To do that brings upon themselves that which man calls sin, for sin is the pollution of his soul, his mind and his heart with the evil power of life.

You have heard that thoughts are living things, and so they are. They do exist as living things. When man uses his thoughts in a deceitful or spiteful or evil way, do not imagine that that is the end of it, for it is not. Far from it. For the thing that you cannot see is evolving by the law that he has submitted into the ethers. For they are clothed in very tiny particles of earthly substance, and a life form is brought into being. That life form is GERMS.

Because they are created from wrong thinking, and the life form had within it that destructive nature, so then, does it attack to destroy the bodies of man.

It was the beginning of disease, and upon it was built, by the linking of other various germs, which had been established by the essence of the Earth itself, different forms of illness according to that part of the body which they attacked.

This is why I say to you, that each of you has within you that power of creation. If you can see how hatred and violence are born on the wings of thought, into the ethers around you, can indeed form germs which too are of a destructive nature, then you will see how the world becomes polluted through the mind of man.

Imagine then, what kind of a world it COULD be, if the thoughts of man were of love, kindness and sincerity. For the same process creation would come into being. Born out of those same thoughts, would be the very antibodies to the evil germ, and would attack the very nature of their existence and subdue them to nothing. THAT LOVE MIGHT REIGN SUPREME.

As the evil thought produces the germ that destroys, and that germ also entering into the Earth itself creating within it disease, so then can the love germ enter into the world, and into the Earth, and bless it with that power of creation. It would embody that very spiritual essence that you can see but cannot touch when you look upon a flower. For the noble child of Mother Nature has been created by God.

Now I know that I appear to be going away from the question that was asked, but unless you have a full background, then you cannot see the true picture. For in those days, when the Lord Jesus entered the world, there was much disease abroad. Therefore, you must have seen, because of what I have just told you - about germs which arise from hatred and evil thoughts, that they were very, very evident in that time, creating all kinds of different illnesses which caused blindness, caused cripples, and all kinds of other diseases which attacked the body.

Imagine then, if you will, the power of that evil that was abroad there, when the Lord came. Had He not come, can you not see how, by this very time that you are living in now, would not even exist, because the fullness of evil would have already been complete, and would have corrupted and killed off life as you know it.

Since your body needs that creative energy that comes from good and from God, in order to be sustained, and the very fruits of Earth that you feed upon need that same light and energy of a creative nature, to supply you with that food, and the very waters that you drink need that same energy of life-giving force to keep it pure and clean for you to drink, can you not see how, had there been no intervention by Christ Jesus, that evil would have multiplied, over and over again, until it got to this point in your time, and there would have been no life as you know it that could exist.

And so, seeing as how those thoughts were created out of sinful ways, Jesus did indeed come, and through the power of His truth and His love, manifested that greater wealth of well-being within those who listened to Him. He didn't quite put an end to the evil thoughts, the evil creator, but created a gap inbetween it. Lifted it up so that it was not totally destructive and insured that there was always those who could fight against it - so that the good thought was always in proportion to the evil thought.

Do you understand that, my children? I am not above you, am I? Then see, that when evil becomes greater than good, it breaks out in the world as wars. That is why you have wars. If you were to turn back and look at those wars which have passed, even in the great second world war, you would find evil at its roots, and by necessity, good had to rise up and overcome it. To put it down.

Had it not done so, had there not been hearts that were stout and true to God, had that good not been there, then the evil would have again taken over the world, and crushed the very free will that you have, and you would not have made any progression. You would have been under the heel of the oppressor. So, whenever that happens, the good must rise up and go into battle to subdue the evil and push it back down again.

If Christ had not come, and said such things as "Love ye one another", "Forgiveness is better than judging and hating", and healed by that wonderful power that came from God, so that He was seen among men as far above them in Earthly terms, then you must see that none of that would have been possible. And so, many people say, and I hear them, "How can Jesus save you from your sins?"

That is the way, but they cannot understand it, neither do they understand what they are saved from. This is the point. For it was God who created man, and He it is who is the Father of us all. You are all His children, growing to become His Sons and Daughters.

When he gave you life forms here, that you might expand your souls with that concept of spirit and love, it was to be for your good, and it was always hoped that man would look kindly upon man, regardless of the colour of his skin, or his nationality, of his beliefs, for you belong to Him. But the ways of evil and him from whom it springs forth, try you, and strive to capture your souls, your minds and your hearts, and make you slaves to darkness. Robbing you of your lives here, and throughout all eternity.

This is something, my children, that you must desperately try to grasp. For Satan is a very wiley bird, and he has many ways of tempting you when you think to yourselves that he is not. But he is. So we say to you always, watch and pray. Watch and pray lest you be ensnared in his ways, and captured, finding yourselves as ones who have become his slaves because you do his will.

So then, what I say to you, is - look towards your life, and what you are prepared to do for that life. For if you are not prepared to fight for it, then you will lose it. I make no bones about this. I tell you, do not think to yourselves that because you come here and call yourselves - whatever it is, that you are safe, you are saved. You are not. The fight is always with you to overcome evil, and it rears its head in many different ways and shapes.

Are there any questions?

Q: So are you saying that Jesus did not come here and die for our sins that we had already committed...

Hafed: Of course He did. I thought I made that quite clear.

Q: It appeared to me that you were saying that He came to save us from sins that we MIGHT commit.

Hafed: And have committed. By raising your thoughts and ideals, so that you change the pattern of your life, and you break free from the chains that bind you to Earth, and to him whose ways are of a destructive nature. That is what I meant.

Q: But does that wipe out the sins that you have already committed?

Hafed: That is so. God does not judge you.

Q: But, if that had been us in that time, when we died and looked back on our lives, would we have been able to forgive ourselves for committing sin even though Jesus had come and forgiven us?

Hafed: Yes, if you had raised yourselves to a level of thought that was in His teaching. Not if you didn't follow Him. If you turned your back on Him and went away, then no. But if you followed Him, and abided in His law and His love, then yes: you would have no regrets to fall back on.

Q: But for those who didn't follow Him, then they would still have to answer for things they had done?

Hafed: Oh yes. Most assuredly. You cannot be something you are not.

Q: Why did He have to die on the cross?

Hafed: In order that man should remember. Had He not died then, and been put to death by man, then I very much doubt whether He would have been remembered, or whether you would have heard any of His teachings.

Q: You have also said that Jesus came to create a gap between good and evil, because evil was about to override good. That is the same now, isn't?

Hafed: That has been very evident for a long time now. You may even be beyond that point now.
Q: So why then has it been allowed to go that far? Why hasn't Jesus come back again before now, or perhaps sent somebody else in His place, rather than later when we have practically destroyed ourselves?
Hafed: God is wiser than me. (Much laughter)
Q: I know! I just wanted to know why! Don't you know why?
Hafed: No, I do not know why. I am like many who come to you with words of teaching, but we cannot answer for the mind of God.
Q: So it is His decision, and He hasn't made it common knowledge. Why?
Hafed: He has not revealed that.
Q: Oh. It strikes me that it is almost like a small child, who, if he has done wrong, might get told off, and you hope that he will learn from that. But the second time, the punishment must be harsher. He didn't get the message the first time, so the second time we have got to be that much harder - and that is what God is doing to us?
Hafed: There is a lot of truth in what you say.
Q: Isn't there also the knowledge of understanding? One person's sin is greater than anothers, because the first person, if understanding these things should not do them, but for the second person who does not understand, the sin is less?
Hafed: That is so. You are right on that point. As I have often said to you, I have not done you any favours, for I have revealed to you the truth, and now you have no escape. You have no hiding place.
Q: There is one thing that I think contradicts itself. When the Preacher came the other week, (another spirit visitor to the group), he told us that when God's children went into the darkness, they were given protection to get people out of the darkness - to bring them to their Father to apologise for their sins.

Now the way I have always understood it, is that if you live on this Earth and you do bad things, when you pass over, you are punished. But these people, they seem to have it both

ways. They do what they like on Earth, then they die, and fair enough they get punished for a while, but then they are let back into the flock, so to speak. Why is this?
Hafed: Can God be any less than your judges who judge a man because he has done wrong, and sent him to prison. Then, when he comes out of prison, he is taken back into the community, and is as one who has committed no offence.

Your Father God does not in any way punish you, your punishment is what you give yourself. It is not Him who throws you into the darkness, He is always pursuing you to come to the understanding of love. And yes, that is why the children of light go into the darker realms, and have been doing so for a long, long time.

I have been there many times to help those who have reached that point where they are ready to understand, but the thing that impedes their progress is mainly the shame they feel when they realise what they have done. They cannot forgive themselves in their hearts for committing wrong when they know they should have known better, but did not. And now is the time, because they have come to that knowledge of God, and come to that full realisation that love is the only way, now is not the time to say, "I am ashamed of myself, I cannot go into the light", for by going into the light they see themselves, and what they have made of themselves. No longer the shape and form that God made, for they have become as evil as sin, and that sin changes them. They become as ugly as that state of being that they find themselves in. That they have created for themselves.

When they come into the light, or the twilight, for that is what it is, they are in such a state of being, that it is terribly difficult for them to progress. For the only way they can do so, is to do good, and there is not the opportunity there for them, and so they make amends by taking on roles in this world, trying to help the needy. Trying to change the ways of man who was very much like them when they were here, or was going to commit suicide.

They have a great fight on their hands, attempting to change and reshape them before they make the change called death, but little by little, because of their fight and their efforts, they change. That evilness that was there, as ugly as sin, gradually begins to fall away, and the gentleness of their new nature begins to form and shine through. Do you understand?

Because God forgave them, that does not mean that they can immediately rise up and go to Heaven. They cannot. For they must be of the same spiritual worth as those who are there.

Q: They are like living forces really - good and evil, aren't they?

Hafed: Yes, very powerful. Very powerful. That is why you must be careful of the way you live your life. Do not imagine that you are avoiding evil all the time. There are those times when you are doing the work of Satan, not the work of God.

Q: What is the definition of Satan? My own definition is that he is not as a soul, a certain person, but what is within oneself, THAT becomes Satan.

Hafed: No, no. He exists. Do not make any mistake on that score. As you have good, so you have evil. As you have a creator of good, so you have a creator of evil. So do not be misled and think to yourself that he doesn't exist, because I am quite certain he would love you to believe that.

Q: Would he be the angel who fell to Earth, who disagreed with Jesus when talking to God...

Hafed: I know what you are going to say. There are many different beliefs and stories, but none of them have any real substance to them. I cannot tell you, It is beyond my time, I am afraid.

Q: Have you followed the case of the young girl in Ireland who was raped, and she was only fourteen? Is there ever a time when abortion is allowed?

Hafed: When you look at this situation, it is no use applying the moral laws of God to it. You must only apply the moral laws of the time to it. For the moral laws of this time are totally out of step with the moral laws of God.

God said: You shall not bear children out of wedlock. God said that a man and a woman come together, and are as one, in marriage. When you look at your world, and see the moral code that exists there, then you can only apply the law according to the standards that man has set himself.

If a man has degraded himself to this degree, then he must live by the law that he has fallen to. It cannot be seen as evil to allow this young girl to have her abortion, for the offence that was committed was against her will. And because a child has been brought forth out of that action that took place, it is no fault of the child, and no fault of the mother. It is the fault of him who committed the offence, and then only because he lives by the moral standards that man has set. Although it is not lawful to rape a woman, it has been a lust which has been raised up within the minds of man because he does not discipline himself or follow the LAW ACCORDING TO GOD.

Also, when you see how some of your women live their lives and dress, it is not surprising that the lust that is there within that man rises to become the beast who comes upon an innocent soul and rapes her.

Now the girl involved - it is her decision. Her decision is for abortion. That means that the child must forfeit its life. But then, she doesn't know this, cannot understand that, and because of her tender years, God would not blame her. No sin will be marked against her.

So we are in this quandary. This indecision, this imperfect state of being that man has fallen to, and created. Had he walked that path that Jesus laid down, it could never have happened. The darkness would never have been in the world to start with. Lust would never have been in the mind of that man, and the women would never have been as they are.

So you have a situation where there is neither right nor wrong, because in a sense, all of them are wrong. No matter what action now is taken, another wrong is going to be done, and in that quandary, the judgement has got to be made by the individual. It can never be the judgement of God, neither can it be the judgement of Jesus. Only love will go to him who created the child by forceful means, she who has passed through this tremendous ordeal, and the child who can find no place in the mother's heart to be given life.

What a terribly, terribly sad situation. It makes you want to cry. I have answered that question to the best of my ability.

Q: Just a point of clarification. When does the child's spirit enter the foetus? Is it at the moment of conception?

Hafed: No. It is in the time when the child first moves. There is a time when the child first moves inside the woman, and that is the point at which the life has been instilled. Up to that moment it has only the life of the body, which is not life in the spiritual essence, as you know it. So when that happens, then the child's spirit is there, and once that happens, that is the greatest damnation if the mother seeks abortion. If abortion can happen before then, the child is not there anyway, it is only a foetus, and there is no sin to any living person.

Q: Is that what is know as the quickening - when the heart beats?

Hafed: That is so. When the child quickens. At about three months. Sometimes they quicken faster than others, but that is when the child IS a child. Before that it is a foetus. It has a life that is like an Earthly life, like flesh has life. The body has a life of its own, but you are the true life that guides the vehicle through life.

But then, the same applies to a child which is conceived and known to be in an unhealthy state because of those who take drugs, or because they have AIDS, or have other forms of illness that prevent the child from living a full natural life. Think about that, for in the case of a child being conceived in the womb of a drug addict or from the sperm of a drug addict, or from a person with AIDS, the child is going to suffer and never have a complete life. There are souls on the other side of life who are waiting to enter the womb of a woman, to call her mother. To have a father who it may call father. To give it life that will best bless it to the growth of spiritual truth. But in this case it cannot be so because the sin has already been committed, both in the case of the drugs and the AIDS persons. The sin would be greater if a soul like I have described, should enter into that foetus, and be trapped for all time, until the body gives up life.

God in His love and mercy, will not permit that to happen either for the mother's sake, the father's sake, or the wrongdoer's sake, because the cross would then become too heavy for them to carry. But there are high souls on our side of life, who say, "Let me go Father. Send me. Let me be the child", and they take on that kind of life. Some of them to a full age, others for weeks, or even hours, but they take it on. Always within that carcass, trapped within that carcass, is a very evolved soul, and they give you a great deal of love. But do not think that that is the only time, and for the only reason. For there are souls on our side of life, whose want and urgent need is to come and be confined, and suffer in a diseased body. That is why many people in your world suffer from diseases, and are never cured, and their pain is terrible. But you do not see their soul when they are risen up from those bodies of torment. You look upon it and see only the suffering, and perhaps you blame God, saying "How could He allow this to happen!".

You see others who are healed by God, and you say, "Why has He chosen to heal this one, and not heal another?" I know that this has been said even by persons in this room. And that is the reason.

Your mind and heart is centred upon the life that you have now. And you feel that your needs are to be happy here, But this is just a small insignificant speck of life compared to where you are going. If it means that you spend that miserable period of time suffering here, in order to be raised up into the full glory of your loving Father, and a life that is vibrating with the true happiness of God, and the gifts of God that He bestows upon you...

You do not know happiness here. You will never know real happiness here. Your life is designed in a way for you to grow in understanding, in kindness and in love, and if you do not, then the price is there to be paid. But you will eventually, hopefully, rise up from that path of degradation, into the loving arms of your Father.

So you can see, there will invariably come a time when things are going to change, as I have said before. Much of the evil ways that are here will be gone. For I have spoken to you about the sufferings of man through the disease that he gets, and it is there for his growth, although not all disease is of that calibre and come with the blessing of God. For there are those diseases that man has created, and we return to that imperfect thought that sets in motion the chain of events that are of a destructive nature. That is not part of God's will, and never can be. But there are those illnesses that come from man, and are there for his own spiritual progression.

Q: Have you, in your long experience of life in the spirit, ever met with an individual who had remembrance of passing through more than one existence on earth?

Hafed: No. If such were the case, I could not say I was myself. I believe I never was on the earth till I was sent direct from the great and mighty source of all spirit. Some men in the spirit world go back to earth, in spirit, and teach the old doctrines they held in mortal life, and which they tenaciously hold. Let such men come and stand on the same platform that I and others occupy, and they will soon learn to think otherwise. Many of us, indeed, return to earth on errands of love and truth, but not in the body.

Q: It is curious we have no mention in the four gospels of Jesus ever referring to his experiences which you you have given in your autobiography.

Hafed: He may have spoken of these for aught I know, but in his interviews with the Jews, it would have been unwise to refer to other nations to buttress up what he wished to impress them, they were so bigoted a people. Hence he would show them from their own sacred writings alone that His mission was from God. It would never have done to refer to such records as those of Persia or Egypt.

Now it is time for me to leave you. I am sorry that I was only able to deal with a few questions, but some were deep questions, and unless I answer them fully, then there is no point in answering them at all.

Farewell.

QUESTIONS & ANSWERS:-

Disbelief in the Divinity of Christ.
"Greater things than these shall ye do..."
Judgement.
Creation of the Universe.
American Scientific recognition of U.F.O's.

Good afternoon and God bless you my children. Peace be with you.

I thought that we might continue with the questions that we began last time I was with you. So, if there is anyone who would like to ask a question of a spiritual nature, then please do so.

Q: I have watched a television programme concerning the hierarchy and the priests of the Anglican Church and their theology and views on the divinity of Christ, and it seems they no longer believe it. Yet they stand there in what I call a frame of mind that is hypocritical, giving the creed as it has been given over the centuries, yet not believing in what they are saying and turning people away from the Church.

Hafed: It is the AntiChrist, is it not? There are quite a number within the Church who do not believe in the divinity of Christ, the miracles, the rising from the dead, or the Virgin Birth, and this stems from the fact that firstly they do not understand what Jesus was or why indeed it was necessary for Him to be born through a virgin. Neither do they understand how it is possible to be raised from the dead, and walk among the living, even though there is testimony to the effect that this is what He has done. Testimony from quite a number of people, not only the disciples but Paul, and also Mary - not the Mother of God, but Mary who was the prostitute and was to be stoned. Do you remember?

She who remained with Him, and was the first to see Him, thinking that He was the gardener. THOSE WHO CANNOT ACCEPT THESE THINGS CANNOT DO SO BECAUSE IT IS BEYOND THE LIMITATIONS OF THEIR OWN

SPIRITUAL AWARENESS. They have grown into a pattern of materialism, and have grown into that belief that nothing outside of natural law within this world can happen, because that is the miracle, and beyond the ability of man.

So without realising it, they have also damned God. For while they would say that they do not believe these things of Jesus, they forget their God and in effect are saying that God cannot do it either. Although they do not say so in as many words, that is what they are saying. If then they believe in God, but not in the miracles of Jesus, why is it not possible for miracles to happen through the power of God? And if that is possible, why is it impossible for Mary to have given birth to Jesus without knowing a man? Why is it not possible that Jesus was raised up from the dead?

If then Jesus is not raised up from the dead, neither is anyone. Or are we saying that it can happen to us, but it was not possible for Jesus? If then it is impossible for anyone to be raised from the dead, the whole of the Bible including the New Testament becomes a lie, for there are no miracles, and no life after death, and their arguments will not stand upon a firm foundation.

If they understand anything about the Lord Jesus, and the fact that He was the Son of God, which they dispute, they would know that the very reason WHY He had to be born through a virgin was BECAUSE He was the Son of God. Because it was God who was His Father. If then you have fathers of an Earthly kind because you are of the Earth, why is it so impossible for Jesus to have a father which is of Heaven, through a virgin? For the very fact that He came among men as the Son of God, made that vital. For if He had had a father of an Earthly kind, then He would not have been different from any other man, for that is the law, and He would have been of an Earthly/spiritual descent, not a Heavenly descent.

How then would it have been possible for Him to do miracles which no other man had done? For would He have not been equal to other men? And would man not have had the right to say, 'Why have you made us unequal? Why have you done this injustice to us?". But it was impossible you see, for that Heavenly power which healed instantly and called forth the dead, to have passed through a carnal body. It would have destroyed the physical body because it would have been too great.

So you begin to see why it was necessary for Jesus to be born not of a man, but of God. For the very body that He had was not like yours. It was more in keeping with that higher spiritual makeup that made it possible for Him to use that great power from His Father, which made it possible for Him to feed the five thousand with so little, made it possible for Him to walk upon water without sinking, and which made it possible for Him to bid the storm cease, and it obeyed.

Have you ever heard of an ordinary man doing these things? If you have, then please let me know. Oh, I suppose it is easy enough to say, "Are these things really true, or are they just a figment of peoples' imagination?". After all is said and done, two thousand years is a long time ago. Things get added and taken away as it is passed from one generation to another. But because the life of Jesus was so important, God has taken care, great care, that that truth has always been maintained right down the corridors of time to this present day.

And so you must think about those who stood and gave their testimony to the fact that Jesus did all these things. Not just His disciples, who many would say were prepared to declare anything about Jesus, so long as they could prove that they were someone special, for that would be totally wrong. You would be forgetting the many thousands who stood and gave testimony to the Lord Jesus, who were not His disciples, but who were the children of God through Him, were persecuted for their belief, and gave their lives for Him over the centuries.

Do you believe then, that they were so ignorant, that they would go willingly to their deaths by being put to the torch, torn apart by wild beasts, when all they had to do was simply deny the existence of Christ, and their lives would have been saved?

If their belief had not been so deep rooted that they accepted as a known fact that Jesus exists and lived, would they have been willing to endure all that, remembering that it was not only themselves that were going to be put to death, but their children also? Man might be prepared in some rare cases to accept his own death for a cause, but he would not sacrifice his children.

It was because they knew that by so doing, their lives would become much richer where they were going. So henceforth, that put down once and for all the question of whether there was a life after death. For if there was none, why did they so voluntarily go to their deaths in the name of Jesus? I do not believe that that could be done. It also makes clear that Jesus had a different birth to you. He had a royal birth, and His father was God. For had it not been so, He could never have done those things that He did, things which were impossible for an ordinary man to do.

I see so many so-called healers in your world, and they say, "Oh there are no such things as miracles' It is just the working of natural law". And yet I fail to see those who are healed by them. I fail to see them walking on water, I fail to see them raising the dead, and yet they have the audacity to say to me that there is no such thing as a miracle, it is just natural law. They say that as if they implement that natural law every hour of the day. So please my children, when you hear such things, turn away, for they are being deceived by those who are manipulating their thoughts. By those who do not come from the realms of light.

I do hope I have been able to answer your question.

Reply: Yes, and a supplementary one as well!

Hafed: Well, it is also written in the reading which you had today, that by Moses came forth the Law, and by Jesus Christ came the Truth and Grace. That is the difference, for the Law can be manipulated by man to mean anything. As indeed you are witnessing even in your world today.

Is there anything further? Are there any other questions?

Q: Your son Dougie (Douglas Arnold), said that Jesus was

with us in the room last week. Can you comment on that?
Hafed: Whenever we journey back from the realms of light, we do not do so alone. We journey back to a room that you meet in every week, and to you it is a confined space, but in reality, in the world of spirit if you like, this confined space is a wonderful temple of light, and the Spirit of Christ sojourns wherever there are those who teach His Truths. Sometimes, that Spirit is far closer than at others, like for example last week, when the Lord's presence was felt very clearly by my son, and He was present here.

He told you these things that you may take heart and feel within yourselves something of that humbleness, to think that He would come and share a moment with you. But He does, and not only in this temple, but also in your lives as well. In your daily work, in your pleasures, in your leisure time, He often draws near. And when you raise your voice in His name, to preach the Gospel of Truth, you will feel His presence much, much more clearly through His love, and you will know He is there. And He does this that you may know that you serve Him.

Have you any further questions?
Q: You said a little while ago, that no human being could do the things that Jesus did, because the power would destroy the body, and yet in the Bible it says that Jesus said, "Greater things than these shall ye do..."
Hafed: Because you believe in Me.
Q: So belief in Him...
Hafed: Does not change anything.
Q: So, if you believe in Him, you could do these things, or an Earthly person could do these things, without changing the body?
Hafed: No. What it meant, was the same thing as you see in the world, whereby in Lourdes a well was formed, and it came forth through faith. The faith of a little girl, and because the people went there and washed, they were healed instantly because it held the Holy power.

When Jesus said, "These things shall you do...", they are being done in some places, not through the individual, but by prayer. If you go to some of these places where healing occurs through priests and other good souls, you will find that it is always by faith and prayer. Yes they lay their hands upon them, but that is symbolic, that does not mean to say that that power comes through them.

Q: So the key to what He said was, "Greater things shall you do in My name".

Hafed: Yes. It is always so. In His name, otherwise you cannot do them. Any further questions?

Q: The Bible is full of paradoxes, isn't it?, and there is one paradox I would like to raise with you, and get your guidance on. Jesus said that if someone does you a wrong, you should go to him and tell him that he's done you a wrong, and if necessary, you should escalate that, I forget the exact text, but you should take someone with you the next time. Yet we are also told, we should not judge. How can you tell someone what you are thinking, if you are not judging them in some way? It also says, 'Turn the other cheek', and there is another paradox there.

Hafed: None of them really are. There is truth in all of them. For you see, when we judge, it means we have committed them to some kind of sentence. But there is another kind of judgement, the one that you do yourself. Meaning to say, that if someone was spreading lies about you which were false and causing you a great deal of harm, it would not be wrong to say that he had committed an offence against you. But that is not judgement, you have told the truth, and you have condemned him to a punishment of some kind. Jesus said that you must go to them and you must tell them, and you must ask them to stop. If they do not do so, then you must take a witness with you, to show that you have done this.

He does all this in order that if you are going to take some kind of action through the law, you are seen to be acting generously by asking that one to tell the truth and say, "I'm sorry, it is lies". That you are not seen to be acting from hate, which is a form of judgement. Hatred is your condemnation of him. But you must be without hatred, for to hate anyone, is also to condemn yourself. For you have caused a great wrong within you, and that will have its reaction upon the physical and the spiritual laws which govern man.

So He is not telling you to judge them, only to judge that he has committed an offence against you, and you go to him and explain this, and you ask him to be honest and declare what the truth really is. That is what that statement was all about. It was dealing with those who in that time would seek vengence rather than forgiveness. Forgiveness should always be there, but their vengeance of course, was to take a life.

So do you understand why He was concerned that they should understand the Law as it was given, and not as man interprets it. What was it that Moses was supposed to have said? - "An eye for an eye, and a tooth for a tooth". But the Lord Himself said, "You have heard an eye for an eye and a tooth for a tooth, which is the old Mosaic Law, but a new commandment I give unto you. That ye love one another, even as I have loved you". Which is forgiveness. And only the Lord can make a new commandment.

Who is this Jesus to give new commandments, if He is only a man?

Any more questions, please?

Q: How does the theory that they are talking about now - How the universe was created, fit in with how God made the world? How does God fit in now that they are discovering radiation waves around the edges of the world, and things like that?

Hafed: It is like this, Many hundreds of years ago, man roamed the Earth, and man looked upon man but didn't know how he worked, for the inners were hidden from his eyes, and he had no knowledge of that which was inside, like the heart, the liver, kidneys and lungs, or what their needs were in order to keep them functioning, But of course, as time went by man delved into the secrets of the body, and discovered he had all kinds of marvellous things packed away inside his physical frame, and all of them had a function. All of them were so vital, in order to keep the man living.

Now, although he discovered all these things, one may assume that because he could not find a spirit there, or love there, that they did not exist. But, you know, he overcame that. For even Darwin's theory could not squash the truth. They never did find the final link between an ape and mankind - and the reason? IT DOESN'T EXIST.

Yes, the caveman had a great deal more hair upon his body than you do, but that transformation took place over the course of centuries, because of the change in the way of life, and the things that you eat and drink. Nothing else.

So you see, we are now at the beginning of trying to discover the universe and how it has been created, and always in the beginning there are a number of explanations. Now the Bible tells us that God created the universe and I KNOW that God created the universe, just as He created you. But as the man of old was incomplete in his assessment of the body when he began, so is man today incomplete in his assessment of how the universe began. And it makes no difference really, you know, because the world will still be there, and so will the universe, and the universe will carry on growing in spite of mans' knowledge, whether it is true or false, or a mixture of both. It matters little.

Let us say then, for example, that the universe was created by a gigantic explosion. Something must have caused that explosion. Regardless of what it was, what kind of gases or compounds came together to result in that explosion, it must have all come from somewhere. They didn't all just present themselves - there has to be somewhere from whence they came. There must have been something that created them. Who are we to say that it wasn't God? Who are we to say then, that the universe did not really erupt and come into being by a gigantic explosion?

But it doesn't mean to say that because that happened, God didn't create it. That can happen in the tiny minds of man, who looked upon the inside of the body of man and found no spirit and no love, and said that God doesn't exist. He didn't make us, because He isn't there. And there were those who fully expected to find something of that nature, in the early days, and did not. As those in Darwin's day, believing it was a chain reaction in evolution.

And so now we are on about the universe, and we are still stuck in that same old frame of mind. The record goes round, still stuck in the same old groove, because really, they want to disprove God!

Q: I was reading in an American magazine of a man who having been involved in a recent discovery, says that he cannot believe the arrogance of man who suggests that God does not exist and is not the source of all creation. It was very interesting.

Hafed: God IS creation you see.

Q: Yes, and at least one man is prepared to stand up for the truth.

Hafed: Yes, because that one man has insight that is greater than most.

Q: I think there are a lot of people acknowledging that there must be a God or a great power behind it, but there are others trying to disprove it.

Q: Because you can't prove it. It's down to faith, isn't it? Its a bit like when you let off a firework in the garden, and there is a bang. You look around for what caused it, and you find the remnants of the firework, and you say that is the cause. But who lit the firework?

Q: I cannot see that there could have been a big bang. I find those two words offensive - big bang. God doesn't work like that, does He?

Hafed: I think that there really was something of that nature.

Q: Do you?

Hafed: Yes. When it happened, and the point is it is still happening today, and God is still creating today, you must realise that the universe is not just the planets that you see, it is also the space that is all around. The planets are only the things that fill the space and void, and that space and void go on and on and on. There is no end, for how can there be? When you come to the end, what will be there? and what will be on the

other side? And that is how you go on. So there can be no end, and that is a miracle in itself!
Q: It's baffling isn't it? In fact, its mind blowing!
Q: God is the greatest scientist of all time, isn't He?
Hafed: And God is, in effect, still creating today, and the point is that man only understands a very small fragment of what the universe represents, and what the plan behind it all really is, and what exists on the other worlds! Just because he (man), can find no one running around in shorts or bikinis, he believes that there is no one there.
Q: They are in a different dimension, aren't they?
Hafed: That's right! Completely! After all, you have fish in the sea, and they don't live like you or me. I live in a different world again, from you or the fish. Mans' mind you see, is too small, and only when it is vastly enlarged, can he understand.

But I know that there is a gigantic plan that is at work in the universe through the creation of all these planets, suns and stars. There is a reason. There is nothing out there that does not have a purpose for being there. Nothing. And you see, you are in effect on a planet, but it is like a giant space craft, for the whole creation of God's planets are moving at a tremendous speed through the universe, as if it were travelling somewhere.
Q: Will the giant plan ever be completed? Is there a foreseeable end to it, or is it something that will go on and on, for ever and ever?
Hafed: I cannot even begin to conceive what lies behind it, or whether it will ever end.
Q: So have you no ideas what the plan is?
Hafed: None whatever.
Q: What I found exciting this week, was the fact that they said flying saucers do exist. One nearly smashed into an aircraft.
Hafed: Oh yes. That is a fact. I think I said that many years ago. I know they do exist, but you must remember, and I tell you again, that not all flying saucers are good.
Q: They say that in America they have captured some sort of craft, and I think that if they (the aliens) were high spirits, they

would not be able to do so. It makes you wonder. The Americans are supposed to have three U.F.O's in hiding, and they are said to be in a museum somewhere. They say they are going to put them on display. They are also supposed to have a body in their possession.
Hafed: Well, I do not wish to continue with that, for in good time you will come to a rapid knowledge of what it is all about.
Q: So its all going to happen in the future. Our future?
Hafed: Oh yes. You cannot avoid that.
Q: Its moving very fast now, isn't it?
Hafed: Oh yes. Very fast.
Q: Would you say that there will be a time in our lifetime when people who are good from other planets will actually come here and communicate with us?
Hafed: I would not know. I am not prepared even to speak on that, to anyone.
Q: Can you elaborate on all flying saucers not being good?
Hafed: I have said so.
Q: There is supposed to be an interplanetary force out in space somewhere, to keep these bad forces outside our range. I do not know how far that range extends.
Hafed: Well, they don't appear to be doing a very good job!
Q: They don't, do they! So there is nothing to your knowledge...?
Hafed: I would probably believe that there is a bad force out there, trying to infiltrate Earth, and they are winning. But I would say that that was more to do with old man Satan!

It is better for you to cast out from your minds all these things which are heresay, fix your minds on the love of Christ, and allow Him to enter your life and guide you, that you may play your part while you are here. For it is better that you serve and accomplish that which you have set out to do, rather than waste your time on negative things which accomplish nothing.

I think it is time for me to leave.

Farewell little ones. Farewell. God bless you, and a safe journey through your life.

WE WHO LOVE YOU MORE THAN YOU KNOW

Good afternoon and God bless each one of you. Peace be with you. It is very often impossible to paint on the canvas of your minds with words, the picture of truth, that you may understand. For according to your own spiritual development and light, so will you draw your own conclusions. Always, there is a difference in those conclusions that you draw.

You have no conception of what actually transpires on our side of life before you come together in one of your circles. Seeing as those who are to come have been appointed to do so by the Lord most high, you could not in any way envisage in your hearts and minds, the overwhelming feeling of joy that is theirs, to know that this is the day they are to return and become an active member of the servants of God. To attend the needs of one who has been placed in their care. Their loving care.

Neither can you see the struggle that goes on with them to free you from your ignorance and your desires, your wrong desires, in order to set you on the true course where the light of God will be in you also Where because you have been lifted out of the darkness, you now stand face to face with them, and are able to be used by your guardian, your teacher.

They know something of the work that lies ahead, and they also know more than anything or anyone, that that work can be so easily destroyed. Everything depends upon the one whom they have been given charge over. For if they turn their face back down the road to that which they used to be, or to where their desires and ambitions lie, it can all so suddenly be turned into sadness for them.

So you can imagine them, my children, something of the excitement that is with us as we journey back here to you. There is a great feeling of joy that springs between us all. As a happy band of pilgrims come back to those they love, and wish so much to raise up from the darkness and despair of their lives into the brightness and joy of God's loving care.

We become as children again when Christmas comes, and it is time to unwrap the gifts. And well you know, you who are parents, that kind of feeling. You have experienced it yourselves from both sides, for you are the parents who have seen it on your children's faces, and also as a child yourselves. So then, is it with us, this happy band of pilgrims who travel back.

You have no conception of how much work is involved in order to make this afternoon possible. You have no conception. You think that all you need to do is to present yourselves, and everything will be alright, but it is not so. For work must be done with you on that morning before you come, and in this sanctuary where you are to receive the wisdom of the healing of God, whether it is your turn to be used as an instrument of truth to give some member of your circle a comforting thought, or be like my son who brought along a reading and told us about love, and how important that word really is.

So we come in love, and very often you have said as you have entered the door, "Isn't it so very peaceful in here? Isn't it so uplifting?". And I have seen you after the circle, when you do not want to hurry away - you linger on, even though you know that the afternoon is gone and the circle is closed. Yet you linger on because you are in a separate world from the one that is your life. The worry isn't there, nor is the anxiety that often fills my little children's minds. I know, because I am often with you, and those who minister to you before you come to the circle, are there to prepare you. To sustain you in all the things that you must do before you attend this circle, that you may prepare yourselves and present yourselves to your Lord and Master as innocent children waiting to be taught, waiting to be bathed in His love.

So you can imagine then, something of all the work that goes on from our side of life in order to give you this opportunity. And it is a wondrous opportunity that we present to you, for we must ensure that while you are here no harm will befall you. No evil can enter, no darkness, no sinful men or women get at you. We must ensure that that Holy power and that wondrous love are your protection.

The greater your ability to love, the greater is the pain of that love when one of you is hurt in any way. You cannot even begin to understand the pain, the disappointment. So you see then, that if that pain is inflicted by the way you live your lives, or because in your flippancy you decide that your pleasure comes first, and you cannot attend the circle, then that is even a greater pain. For WE are the ones you inflict the pain upon. WE WHO LOVE YOU MORE THAN YOU KNOW. WE WHO CARE FOR YOU MORE THAN YOU KNOW. We who suffer far greater, in order to protect you against the evils of your time - we stand and block the evils that would come. We receive the blow, not you.

So the promise that you come with in the first days, those early days of your youth - youth meaning not the body, but the youth of the new found spirit, the bloom of it begins to fade, and the light of the world becomes even stronger, so our hearts grow even heavier, We wish for you to know this,

When there are those who are absent in your circle, you cannot see the disappointment of those who love them, and who come to tend to them. You cannot see the disappointment that they wear on their faces, especially if the absence is unnecessary. Then it is more than a disappointment, it is almost like a disgrace between your spirit colleagues, that you have been unable to bring your child to the altar of God on this afternoon.

I am telling you all this, because I want you to be conscious of the dedication that lies behind your circle, and those who minister to you. I want you to be concerned about it, because when the absenteeism grows in your circle, we cannot protect you like we should, and we too grow weary and worry as to how this might be accomplished. It is not as easy as you think, for you only know what you see about you. You do not know what lies behind you.

And so you must realise the importance of the work that we are striving to bring you to do. You must realise for your own safety's sake. There are none of you here who could say to us that this circle this afternoon is as you would have liked to have remembered it. That you do not miss those who are not here, because all of you do, and you know it is not the same.

If you are to become the servant of God, it is to be with the same dedication as those who minister to you. For they have only the best to give, and therefore you must be prepared to give the best of yourself also. I tell you that there is nothing more important in your life than to be here on a Saturday afternoon. Nothing,

You cannot see this, I do not expect you to. You will not see it until you have made the change called death. Then, standing with us and looking back, you will see, and if it ever becomes your task to become a guardian to a soul on Earth, and have that soul entrusted to you, to bring them to the flower of their spiritual youth that they may serve the Master, then you will understand. You will know what I mean,

In the scriptures, in the reading that you had this afternoon, were given a very clear indication of what you are working towards. That you walk in the light of God, and it is the love of God that is your protector, your guardian, as you walk through life.

The gifts of the spirit are given only to those who are the servants of God. Is this not what it says? For the carnal man cannot receive those gifts. They are foreign to him, He cannot understand them, neither can he abide them. He cannot live by that law, for he does not understand. This is why you walk by the love of God, for many there are who cry out that they are the servants of God, but few there are who truly are. To say one thing, is quite different from actually being

Many say it, in order to find praise in the eyes of their fellow men and women. To stand on a pedestal that others might look up at them and say, "Isn't she marvellous, look at what she is doing", when in her heart there is not a true love there, or the true dedication.

It is always those who do these things and say nothing, who are the true servants of God. And as you walk through your life, the love of God gives you that protection against faltering in your ways, Against the ambition and desires and obsessions that come from our side of life, from the darker forces, who oppose you because you do the will of God. But the love of God is protection against these things, and if that is with you, then your road is straight and you will not falter. Your joy will be assured, and your happiness will be complete. You will have a place in your Father's house, where happiness and contentment is in abundance.

You will travel far and wide throughout the universe, throughout the realms of spirit, in His name. As you do so, so you will learn and grow in stature. In that stature of love, and in that likeness of God, your Father. For do not your children grow up in your likeness - the likeness of the parent? So then do the children of God grow up in His likeness.

I ask you to keep these things in your minds. I ask you to consider them, to realise the frustration that those who love you go back with, if they have come and given you the words of spiritual comfort, and yet because you are doubtful as to whether it is right or wrong, will not rise and speak what you have been given.

Neither do you know the joy that comes with them on their return when that one whom they have come to teach has stood up and gives what they have instilled within them. Then there is a joy with them, because you have taken the next step. And if you can do this once, my children, then you can do it every time that you come. And every time that they tend to you, they will open your mind a little wider, and give you something completely different. As you grow, so you will become aware, constantly aware of their presence, as they enter your aura and bring with them the sweetness of their love.

Now for you, my children, a Saturday morning should be a time that is filled with excitement and anticipation, because you know that you are to come here in the afternoon. If you feel like this, then you are linking truly with those from our side of life, who impart to you that special gift of love and enjoyment that you give to your teacher. But if it has become a duty, if it is that your heart is heavy because you feel that you must be there and yet your heart and minds are in a different place, then you should not come.

I realise that there is always the exceptional occasion when you will wish to be somewhere else, or their will be a special event, and we accept that, but when that happens too often, when you seem to be enjoying yourself too much to want to come here, then is the time to stop and question why you do. For it would be better to part, and say I have tried but I can go no further. we will understand, there will no bitterness with us. We will understand, and we will wish you well in all that you intend to do.

There are always those who wish to come, want to come, desire to come, that they may have the opportunity that has been given to you. So there will be no question of depletion within the circle, there are always those who are waiting to come along and serve their God.

We do not want you to think or believe that you are held here in chains, for that is far from our cry. That is far from what we wish to teach you. For always we speak of freedom. Freedom of the soul. That is why you have free will, and that is why you must continue to use your free will. But do not use your free will in believing that is a duty for you to perform. It is not. It must always be an act of joy, a feeling of excitement because - this afternoon I am going to my circle, and this afternoon I am going to be linked with my teacher and with all those who come with him. Friends and helpers, they all will be there, and we will feel something of their world, and be taught something about our heavenly Father who created us.

If this world is to be raised up, and saved from its agony, pain and misery, then it must be through those souls such as yourselves, who will stand up and be counted, and without fear, deliver the truth. Even though it may mean that you will suffer at the hands of those who oppose you, both in this world, and in the world to come.

That is the challenge that is there, and I have never tried to deceive you as to the difficult path that you have chosen, and as to the dangers that lie along that path. I have never, ever tried to deceive you. This is why I have emphasised to you in the past to consider your love for each other, your care, and how you should pray for each other, for these are the very reasons why. How you must live your life so that you will not attract the wrong kind of people to you, and involve those in your circle with that kind of danger, because you are all interlinked.

And so beloved, do not think that I have come to scorn you, I have not done that. I have come to give you a measure, if you like, of our love for you, and our needs that you must supply to us in order for us to accomplish our work in you.

You see, our heavenly Father has sent us on a mission, because He has a plan - a wondrous plan, to bring salvation and redemption to His children, and you are part of that plan.

When you were in the spirit, and before you were born, you were enthralled with the idea that you had been chosen to go! And we knew you, and we spoke with you, and we taught you as much as we could, so that you may have some kind of light and strength when the time came for you to face the very tasks that we had sent you about. You can surely see this. You can see how many have been lost to us over the course of time, and because they have been lost to us, they are lost to themselves. When their time comes to return home to their God, can you imagine what tears there will be. When they stand before the noble soul and say to Him, "Father, I have failed". You have no conception, my children, of what that means. None whatsoever

And so, without further ado, without anything else to be said, I would like to say to you also, something of the pain that is felt too, by my son (Dougie Arnold) who I use. It is not easy for him. He knows through past experience how difficult a way it all is. Especially if you are a teacher like him, who comes with that same love for you, and that same desire to set you free, that you may walk in the same light as he has shared. Yes, his pain is there too.

When you have one among you who is a teacher, then you should care for them, very carefully. For you know not how fortunate you are. Give double thought and consideration to all you do within the circle, and in your friendship with each other, and for him who stands as a doorway for you to enter into your Father's house. When you are ready you will enter, and when you enter, it will be because he has given so much, that you may do so.

Farewell my children until we assemble again. I am sorry that it was not the subject I had intended to speak to you about, but it would be unfair to those who had missed it, and gave me the opportunity to implant something within your hearts and minds that perhaps you had never seen.

Farewell, farewell.

LIFE IS MORE THAN YOU KNOW

The growth of a tree is known by its height. The height of a man is known by his works. And the works of a man are known by his labours. So says the teacher.

I greet you beloved, in the name of love, and in the name of Him who I call Lord and Master. Peace be with each one of you.

It is always a very satisfying, time to come to you in this sweet hour, and join your mind to ours, that for a little while we may be able to talk upon great and small matters. For well I know your need to learn, well I understand the capacity within you to put those teachings into your life and make them work for you. Well I understand how difficult it is for some, and how easy it is for others who can see more clearly the ways of God and find within themselves a deeper and more sincere form of love.

All things are not from God. Only those things that grow in beauty, and prevail over the ugliness of mans' life that he creates for himself, and which is self-inflicted.

The joy of knowing God, is found in the knowledge of God. To say I believe, I know God. He is one who lives and dwells within me, and has His being in my life, because I decree that it should be so. I know God, because when He comes, His love fills every corner of my mind, and my heart is filled with joy.

So it is before you then, my children, not the most difficult of tasks to learn, neither is the lesson set before you one where you need to be able to use words, for words are just what they say - words.

But the lesson that is set before you is seen by the soul, the inner eye. Understood by the spiritual mind, never understood by the carnal mind. It is one that you see through the spiritual gifts that God has invested in each one of you. It comes to you more by feeling and knowing, than it does in any other form. It is a way in which you grow. Grow in enlightenment to be who you say you are - the children of God, becoming likened to that child that God wishes you to be and loves all the more because you try and place yourselves upon that path or light.

Love then beloved, is your servant. Let it come and serve you. For a man's servant comes to his master each morning to dress him, so then does love come to you, to dress you in that garb of spiritual beauty that it may reveal to you that greater light of truth, that in itself may reveal that great and wondrous joy that becomes your happiness in all things.

Do not doubt, for while I may say to you that there are many things for you to doubt in, because the world presents those things in all the ugliness that man spawns upon the world itself. Do not doubt, because doubt belongs to ignorance, and you cannot see beyond the life that you have. But in that truth, let it become your eyes for tomorrow. Let yourself be free from the fears that chain you to life in all its many forms of prison that come from fear. Love has nothing to do with any of these things.

Do not fear for tomorrow, for tomorrow is but one day, and it will come and go just like yesterday, and no one can prevent it from happening. But rather look towards the life that is yet to be. For here is the fulfillment of all the things that you hope for. There, my children, in company of all those who love you well, will you journey on beyond realms of this world, with all its troubles, fears and doubts, into a clear awakening of who you really are.

For love comes as a servant to you, and dresses you in all that apparel which is of the royal family. For that is who you are. You are the princes and the princesses of the realm, for you are the Father's children, are you not? And whoever it is who comes to Him in love, and asks to be received, shall not be turned away, but will instead be fed the bread of Heaven that it may sustain you throughout your life.

You are buffeted on every side by those who oppose you, both from the realms of darkness, and those who are yet in the body, and are the servants of those in the realms of darkness. They torment your minds with doubts. Doubts about your future, doubts about your beliefs, but fear them not, for the love of God has overcome all of them. But rather be a child, humble in every way. Set your crown of life in the forefront of spiritual truth, that you may gather to yourself all the wisdom that is there to be found. Let it reveal to you the life that is yet to come.

For I say to you that very few there are who even understand what that life is to be. They cannot comprehend the mighty change that takes place with all of you. A change so great, that you will look back and wonder at yourself for allowing the world to chain you so closely to the doubts, fears and evils that abide there.

Can you then imagine that newness of life where you are changed from the man that you are now, from the woman that you are now, into a new being, into a being that lives a different kind of life. Not one that needs a place to abide, like a house to live in. Not one where they need a place to work or to prosper, or to grow in their ambitions and see them fulfilled, but a newness of life that has never been known to you before. A freedom of life that you have never experienced before. No boredom for you. No worries about how you are going to achieve this or that. For all of your time will be filled with the truth of the new life that you have come to. Not the life that is first given to you in the astral world, but the life that lies beyond there, in those other higher realms. For as you go on to each one, you lose that part of you that clung to something of the Earth. As you grow freer, so you embrace new ideas, new concepts. You become embodied with a greater power, a greater freedom, where you will travel wherever you wish in your Father's kingdom.

For those who love you most, and were your teachers before you ever came here in life, journey with you to teach you the way and show you the lessons that you must learn in order to grow and fulfill your part in that wondrous new life. There are no words I can use which can begin to explain it. There is no understanding here of a life like that. It is beyond the imagination of man. And all these things, my children, are there for you in the future.

But what is it that you must do, in order to reach that place? You must hold fast to the truth that has been revealed in you. You must strive to fulfill the Law of God, the spiritual law at work within you. For only that law that is at work within you, can purify your body, your mind and your soul, and set you free from every dark thought, every dark seed, that has been sown within you.

For when man hears of these terrible events that take place in this world, do they not cry out against them? And yet quickly they forget, quickly do they accept what has happened. Those who do not do this, hold fast to this - seeking for revenge, which is a poison that is within them, and can bring greater suffering to others if it is allowed to rule in your world.

Many there are who seek to know the truth, who have arrived at that place where they realise that there must be something more than what they know, and they wait along the road of life. They are waiting for you. They are waiting for you to bring them that knowledge that will set them free. The love that will give to them that joy of living. The peace that will drive away their fears and anxieties. They wait for you.

This is the road then that you must walk first, before you come to your Father's kingdom and take your place in that realm. For you must do your works. You must perform your acts of charity and mercy. You must reveal the secret word that is locked up within you. That secret word of life eternal. You must teach that it is better to love than to hate - a lesson that they cannot appreciate at the moment because of the darkness and fear that fills their minds, a darkness that has been sown within them because of their current lifestyle.

You then, are to set them free. But what if you fall away by the wayside and are taken up with doubts and fears yourselves of this life that you live? - concern yourselves too much with your own ambitions and desires? Shall you still be there to greet them and hand them that precious gift of eternal life?

For life eternal is only good to those who can be free from the pain, and saved from the gates of hell. Life eternal only becomes a joy, when you know your God. When you know the salvation that lies in the truth that is given to you.

If a man is obsessed in some way or another with an evil thing, his obsession will give to him great pain, and he will know that it is from that obsession that his misery springs. But he will not be able overcome it unless he has the weapons to do so. Unless he can find a conqueror to come to his rescue. Unless he can find a great strength that will overcome his weakness. Unless he can find the truth, and comes to the knowledge of God. The knowledge of life eternal, and the ways of love as his servant.

If he can find all these things, then he will break the chains that hold him, and overcome. Because his great strength will lie in the love of his God, and the love of all mankind. He will set his feet upon that path of service, whereby he may go forth to rescue others who even then are held fast by that obsession that once held him.

My children, none of you are free of one obsession or another. You are all bound in some way. You are all caught up in the web of Earth, and the mist and the darkness that lies before you in life, prevents you from seeing beyond. Prevents you from coming to this great strength and determination to overcome and wipe away your tears, your heartache.

LIFE IS MORE THAN YOU KNOW, my children. Much, much more. You are only thinking on the surface of life. You are only scratching the surface. In your belief, you consider that life is the very joy of living, and it depends whether you are able to live your life in the lap of luxury, or the lap of poverty. For both are different sides of the same coin.

If you spend all your time in pursuit of one or the other, you will lose the God-given time that was given to you to seek for your salvation. For your salvation and your true happiness do not depend upon either of them.

Look at the world, and other men of different nations, who in their poverty and ignorance steal, murder, rape and become drunkards, drug addicts. That is their way of life. Do you not feel a great sadness for them, because they do not understand? Or do you think to yourself, it is their own fault, they chose that way.

DID they choose that way? Or were they left with no other alternative because man was too greedy to see their misery, and having no compassion within him, left them to their own devices.

There is no country in your world that you can look to and will not find a measure of this evil growing up like a web, entangling the lives of many. And even those who think they are above it, who think they are free from it, are the very least who should be so confident. For they are the very ones who are the real danger. Real danger my children, of losing all that they have.

To those who wish to live by the law, it is there for them. But it is no use speaking about mans' law, for it is bought and sold on the market places of the world. But I speak about God's Law. God's Law is formed within you. Not within the world, but within YOU it becomes alive. Yes, for it is the only way to guard yourself against the evils of your time. You cannot be touched if that Law abides within you.

When you make the change called death, and rise to the higher spheres, then my beloved, you do not need the Law, for you know what is right. You know that it is due to those who are less fortunate than yourself, and you give all you can that they might receive. What you are giving is not bread and water, it is not a coin of the realm, it is not a position of great height, but more than that. You are giving them the very seeds of life that they may live by.

So all of this then my children, what you are gathering to yourselves now, is for nothing, and all my works that I have given to you will come to nought, if you fail to take up that sword of truth and do battle with the enemy of man. It lies within your path, within your domain, you must choose what you will. I can take you no further. What you must do now must be in your own interest, in order that you may be there at that right time when one seeks for God, who is hungry for His love, and asks you to give him a morsel of food from the Lord's table.

There I will end, and I will give the rest of the time to questions that you may have. If you have any questions, then please ask them and I will do my best to give answers to you.

Q: What if some people just don't want to be helped? What do we do then?

A: Nothing. You cannot help those who do not want help. You must wait until they find the truth. Until they get to that point where they know they need help. When that happens, then they will ask. But until then there is nothing you can do but pray for them.

Any other questions? Are you clear on all points - have nothing to ask?

Q: I am clear on everything, but the question is, would I be able to do it? It's so easily said, but how strong are we?

A: You are as strong as your love that binds you to God. As for saying whether you could do it or not, I think in many ways you are already doing that, are you not?

Q: Sometimes. But you seem to do it without realising, and when you came face to face, you seem to back off wondering whether you can do it.
A: That is the hesitancy that comes from not knowing, of having that little bit of doubt within you.
Q: Thank you.
Hafed: I wish you to know, as I wish you all to know, that when you go into service to God, and you help or try to achieve something for someone, do not believe that you are alone, or that it is left for you to do by yourself, for it is not. There are legions of soldiers, and when I speak of soldiers I do not mean those who fight in wars, but I speak of those who fight for truth and love, and the souls of man, and they are there to help you.
Q: I think many times brother, of the souls in the third world. The little ones who are suffering so very much at this time. I feel so helpless towards this. I know I can pray, I do pray to help them, but I feel that it would help me to feel stronger in myself if I could only do what you did and others like you in your time on Earth, when you walked from country to country helping many souls personally.
Hafed: You must realise that in my time, the world was different from the world in which you live today, and that I had no responsibilities towards wife or child. I had myself to look to, and as long as I could keep it like that, it did not matter to me whether I died or lived. It was by the will of God that these things were done. Even as it is by the will of God as to whether you will survive the night. You understand me? All these things are by the will of God. And in that time there was not the way of life that you have, where you have to go to work, where you have to pay your rent and live in houses. Nothing like that.

I could lay my head upon a rock with a canopy of the stars above me, and I was at home and I could sleep. My needs were very small. A portion of food here, a drink of water there, but nothing more. It was far better that I carried the word of truth that enriched the souls of man than it was that I should think of anything else. If a robber came upon me and took my life while I slept, it was the will of God. If a wild beast had jumped upon me and taken my life, it would be the will of God, and it was not for me to argue with the Lord. If He had let me go forth and accomplish my mission, then that too was the will of God. And as I with my colleagues took to the Lord Himself those gifts of the spirit, that too was the will of God.

And so you see that perhaps there are things in your time that you can do, even though you are restricted so much. You give welcome to those who are in need of healing. You speak that word of truth to those who will listen. You have a generous heart and a praying mind. What more then my son?

Q: Its Just that I feel I want to do more!

Hafed: Then perhaps you will. Who is to say what the will of God is?

Q: I don't want to be tied to my own country really, but if I am, so be it.

Hafed: The children of God are in every country, my son, and their needs are just as great in their own way, as are those in the third world. Remember that those in the third world have not known the way of life that you have, and so it is no great lose to them. But those here, who find themselves homeless and hungry and with fear, they have known these things, and so the suffering is equal.

Any more questions?

Q: When all the pop groups of the Earth got together and raised millions of pounds for the children in need and for other countries, the lorries carrying the relief were stopped and things were stolen, and it just breaks your heart to see this go on - even the governments took so much.

Hafed: I know what you mean, sister, but it is not really a question. I can see your anguish with it all, but then, that is the way of man. Any other questions?

Q: Can I just clarify? Are you saying we should be purely reactive to people who come to us, or are you saying we should go further than that and search out these poor souls? If its the latter, when will the spiritual point in our education be

reached when we are able to do that? You told us not long ago that we are still in kindergarten.
Hafed: That is so, and it is my hope that you reach beyond the kindergarten. But I also said that they wait down the road to meet you on the tomorrow. I did not say today, next week, this year, but down the road. When you have gathered all that your Heavenly Father has to give you, in wisdom and in song, and in joy and in love, that makes you able to go to them. Or when they have come to you and you give them what their needs are.

Just as each one of you here today - did you not all come with a need? Did you not all seek me out to find you an answer? Were you not in that same position at one stage or another? Then he who I use now, and call my son (Douglas Arnold), he was there to meet you, was he not? Who would have known where your lives would have gone had he not been there to say to you, 'My son, my daughter, come this way. For Utopia is not where you search, and I will show you a different way'. Had he not have done that for you, where would you have been I wonder?
Q: Lost in the wilderness.
Hafed: But here you are, and all we ask of you is that you do not give us anything in the way of worldly things, just that you be there to give others the same as we have given to you.
Q: You are looking for commitment, aren't you? You are looking for deeds rather than words.
Hafed: I am looking for deeds rather than words. Not just talking, but action is what I require. And the first action that I need from you if you are to be there when the need arises in those whom you will talk to you must be the first. This is the prime importance of it all. You must be there first to receive what you are going to give to others who wait down the road. Do you understand me my children? Then you must agree that there has been a lot of absenteeism, and I worry over this, because it is a fact that, like the saying says - 'Absence should make the heart grow fonder', but I fear the other saying which also says 'Out of sight is out of mind'.

Q: I feel that from now on members will be attending more regularly.
Hafed: I want to get you all together again, so that we can resume that pathway that we once began to tread, for it is needful, it is necessary, and I only have a certain time that is allotted to me. I cannot go beyond that time because my son will no longer be present with you, for he too must journey on. And so you see, there is a need for haste, need for concern, to receive the gifts of the spirit, that we who labour with you in this sweet way may fulfill all that which He whom I call Lord and Master has sent me about, and that my son may have finished the painting of his works, that we too may hang our painting in that great hall of works.

So be still within yourselves, and let the measure of God enter. Let His love come and be your servant. Let His truth be raised up within you as your companion along the road of life. Be still and know that He is God, and that with Him all things are possible. Do not fear death, even though it may come along the way. For death is a great joy to many, and a great fear and anguish to others. But you will find the joy before the anguish.

And so my children, I leave you for now, with these thoughts, hoping that they may take root within you, and spring up as a full understanding of the work that lies there before you.

Read again the chapter from Romans 8, starting at verse 18. Read it, take it in, because it is true and beautiful for all of you. For you too must become the adopted sons and daughters of God, if you are to become the princes and princesses of the realm.

Farewell my children, farewell.

* * * * *

Reading: Romans 8 v 18.
I consider that the suffering of this present time is not worth comparing with the glory that is revealed to us, for the creation

waits with eager longing for the revealing of the sons of God. For the creation was subjected to futility, not of its own will, but the will of Him who subjected it in hope, because the creation itself will be set free from its bondage, to decay and obtain the glorious liberty of the children of God. We know that the whole of creation has been groaning to travail until now, and not only the creation, but we ourselves who have the first fruits of the spirit groan inwardly as we wait for adoption as sons, the redemption of our bodies. For in this hope, we were saved. Now hope that is seen is not hope, for who hopes for what he sees? But if we hope for what we do not see, we wait for it with patience. Likewise, the spirit helps us in our weakness, for we do not know how to pray as we ought. But the spirit Himself intercedes for us with sighs too big for words. And He who searches the hearts of men, knows what is in the minds of the spirit, because the Spirit interceded for the saints according to the will of God. We know that in everything God works for good with those who love Him, who are called according to His purpose. For those whom He foreknew, He also predestined to be conformed to the image of His Son, in order that He might be the first born among many brethren. Those whom He predestined He also called, and those whom He called He also justified. Those who He justified, He also glorified.

What then shall we say to this? If God is for us, who is against us? He did not spare His own Son, but gave Him up for us all. Will He not also give us all things within? Who shall bring any charge against God's elite? It is God who justifies. Who is to condemn? Is it Christ Jesus, who died? Yes, who was raised from the dead. Who is at the right hand of God. Who, indeed, intercedes for us. Who shall separate us from the love of Christ? Shall tribulation or distress or persecution? Or famine or nakedness or peril or sword? As it is written, for Thy sake we are being killed all the day long. We are regarded as sheep to be slaughtered. Knowing all these things, we are more than conquerors through Him who loves us, for I am sure that neither death nor life, nor angel nor principality, nor things present nor things to come, nor powers nor height nor depth, nor anything else in all creation will be able separate us from the love of God in Christ Jesus our Lord.

THE ROAD HOME

I greet you beloved, in the name of God, and in the name of Him whom I call Lord and Master. Peace be with each and every one of you.

When I was with you last week, I believe I spoke to you of that which gave people two choices. That which was good, and that which was ill, and that was in truth, a fair extent on mans' free will. That with it, the theme of one or the other runs through everything that you do in life. Every choice that you make, the theme of one or the other is in it.

It may seem strange for me to say, that the hardest path in life to follow, is the one that leads you back home. For you have no memory of this home, unlike the memories that you carry with you here where you know your home. And when you have been away, perhaps on holiday, or indeed visiting friends, how often have you said, "I'll be glad to get home and have a nice cup of tea". I am sure that many of you here have said that.

That to you, my children, is your home. Even though you dwell in a strange land, you have made your home here. But when you make the change called death, and return to your REAL home, you shall be greeted in the foothills of God's kingdom by those who love you, have served you, and have served with you in life. And yet, in order to go home, you must have faith.

Faith comes in many different forms. It is not only a faith in a God you cannot see, but a faith you must have in yourself. In your own ability, in your own accomplishments. For many times you say, "Oh no, I could not do that". And yet you can, by faith.

Faith always seems to be required when the task that you undertake is not seen - is hidden from your eyes. Whether it is having faith in your own abilities to accomplish things that you desire, or whether it is in that faith in others whom you call friends and loved ones. Or whether it is in your ability to choose the right way in life. To do what is right.

Not always an easy task, for you are very often badgered by your own desires, your own frailties within you, your own weaknesses that sometimes are there like an obsession to you, and always those things are for the 'ill' never for the good. And yet, it is only faith that can give you the strength to overcome that shallow part of your life, that will in the long run never provide you with that spiritual comfort and wealth that to do the right thing, would.

I realise that it is difficult enough to do the humdrum things in your world right, and to choose to stand up against those who would oppose you, because your ways are not their ways. Because you stand up and say there is no death, life is eternal, and those souls come back to us from the world in which they now dwell. And I know that there are so many who oppose you, because you say that.

But if it is true, and you believe it to be so, what do you do? Do you stand up and oppose those who speak lies? Or do you for the sake of peace and quiet, or perhaps fear of them, agree with them and silently say, 'I will agree with them, but I know that it is not true', little realising that when you do this, you are opposing God. You are challenging the truth that He has given to you.

And when all is said and done, it comes down to this. Are you really worthy of the truth that you have? Do you know exactly what it demands from you? Do you understand that if it means that because you stand to defend the truth you will forfeit your life, then that is what you must do?

There is no sitting on the fence. There is no agreeing with the opposition. There is no back-tracking. You have been given the truth. What do you do with that truth? Do you shroud it in darkness and keep it hidden? For then you would have been worse than those who oppose you. For they oppose you, believing that they are true. In their ignorance, they do not know that in your wisdom, you do know, but through fear, do not trust God sufficiently to cry out loud what that truth is, that light through your efforts, may be born in the minds of others.

So we come to this word - trust, do we not. And we find, in this trust, there is the same measure of faith to believe, to have confidence, to trust one another. You have a circle, and within that circle, there lie your companions in arms. For they, by the very fact that they are here, cried aloud that they are soldiers for Christ. That they will raise their swords of truth and smite the enemy. Dumbfound him with their words of truth and salvation.

Have you all got that conviction? Have you all got that courage? Do you all bear that same hallmark of Christ of which we have been speaking? - as has been invested in you? Or is it just something that goes into your mind and you say, "Lovely! Beautiful words! I love to listen to it!"

But the reward is not for him who listens, but for him who carries the banner into the enemy camp. That is where the reward lies. You must therefore, have trust in each other. For in that trust, there lies your strength. You can only be as strong as your weakest link, and faith, my children, must not be "I think", but I KNOW that there is a God, and He knows me.

Does that surprise you? - that God knows each one of you personally? That you are known by name. Does that really surprise you? But why should it? For when you were home, living with your Father in His mansion, you knew Him, and you knew His name. That is why I said to you that you were to go home. These other homes that you have erected in a strange land are just for your temporary comfort and convenience. For you, my children, are the princes and princesses of the realm of God. The true king.

Weekly you come here, through those doors into this sanctuary of love, light and healing, bearing the dross of this world from your life, and as you assemble here, so those who love you dearly, work hard to relieve you of that, for we know that it is an illusion which you wear, and we do not want you to suffer with illusion, but to see clearly through the eyes of faith what is fact and truth.

While here you listen and are inspired. You walk a little taller when you pass out of that door, and you think to yourself 'Things seem a lot clearer now, things are a lot brighter', but as the days pass and you continue with the daily routine, so those things that brought you to the very threshold of the great God, begin to slip away, and your eyes once more are filled with the things of the Earth and the promise of the Earth, and the things which you think you need but do not, for they are the very things which we are seeking to free you from. The illusion of life is very strong, and can lead you so very easily along that pathway of evil and darkness.

Many of those in your world who you rub shoulders with day by day, are there walking in darkness. Darkness of their own mind. And yet still they are brothers and sisters, and still must come the day when they are set free, but you don't want to heed their way and fashion your life and thoughts on their ways, or model your desires along the pleasures that they find through the flesh. For I tell you that only misery lies there as a reward for you.

But on that road to Heaven, on that road back home, lies that perfect insight of true contentment and happiness, and you are being bound together, hopefully through the strength of our words that we give to you, in the Law of God, in love, in understanding, in trust to each other, that you may be filled with the zeal of God and cry out to do His service for your brother, that you may be able to paint the same true life story on the canvas of their minds, as I have painted on yours. To give them the opportunity to free themselves from the misery and drudgery of life, that they choose for themselves by taking the wrong road, because of the bright lights and the attraction which is just an illusion fashioned and modelled in their desires of the flesh, and nothing more.

When you look back over the centuries, and read about the kind of things which happened in your scriptures, and see how all these things were won by faith, it will not be any different for you. You will find it no more easy than they. Many things which we tell you, you have got to take on trust, having faith that we do not design such things to lead you astray. We try, through logic, to appeal to the insight of your minds, that you may say to yourselves, at least it is logical.

For we have to ask you to believe that you are going home, and that there is a home for you. We have to ask you to believe that we are the sons of light that journey back to make you the sons and daughters of light.

Light is the only form of freedom and contentment that you can have. Darkness and sin will wear you down to the very bottom of the pit. We are the sons of light. We appeal to you through the words we bring believe us, trust us, and have faith in us. Not only in us, but more so in Him who has sent us, that you may become just as close and at one with Him as we ourselves. Consider then your life, and choose what is right. Remember that what has been given to you, is not just for your sakes, but for the sakes of all others who will listen, and are ready to receive that truth.

Well, it is also written that by Moses came forth the Law, and by Jesus Christ came the Truth and Grace. That is the difference, for the Law can be manipulated by man to mean anything, as indeed you are witnessing even in your world today.

Now my children it is time for me to leave you. God bless each and every one of you. Farewell.

THE MIRACULOUS POWER OF LOVE

A lesson for you to learn.

Jesus said, "If you have faith such as a mustard seed, you could say to the mountain - be cast into the sea, and it would obey you".

Here lies a miracle, the same as many other miracles of healing, walking on water, forbidding the storm, and raising the dead, and yet it seems, all that we need is faith such as a mustard seed, to be able to perform a miracle. Yet, my children, there is something missing from the completion of the miracle that could occur with faith such as this, and that is love.

For a miracle is a work that has been done by love. For it is by the power of love that these things occur. For God IS love, you see. And the greater the love that you have within you, the greater is God within you also. And you are His children, sons and daughters to be. Therefore, you yourselves are miracles. A living, walking, talking miracle.

And He has placed within you the ability of creation, for you too can create. Not only in a physical sense, when a child is born, but in a spiritual sense as well.

You create by clothing your thoughts with love in such a positive manner as to know that it shall be so. But you can accomplish nothing of this, except that the love of God be so strong within you. That is the vital key that you need.

Our words to you over the course of time are to be so designed as to make it possible for each of YOU to do miracles. To bring you to that full awareness of God, and who God is, and who you are.

I want you to see that there are not only miracles of life, but miracles of darkness too. For a man reaches out his hand and takes a life, and that is a miracle. That he has taken a life. One designs an instrument of war to kill and maim, and that too is a miracle, a miracle of destruction, because it is in the power of man to create and to do.

If a man then is so full of miracles that are of a destructive order, why then has he never been able to use that same power for good?

There are many types of miracles, my children, from the very smallest, to the greatest. A child crying is an example. The mother picks up the child and comforts it, and the child ceases to cry. That is a miracle. A heart is broken because someone they love is no longer with them, and then in a little while, that someone appears again in their life and takes away their broken heart, mends it and brings them joy. That also is a miracle.

There are many types of miracles. All miracles that are bound up in good, are what you, my children, are striving to do in your Father's name. You are striving to take His holy power and bring about a miracle by your love.

A person comes to you and they are filled with doubt and fear, and, with your love and reassurance, their fears disappear. That is a miracle. You place a seed in the soil, and from it springs forth the fruits of the earth. That is a miracle. And there are none that can deny it.

A miracle is love. A miracle itself is the work that is done by love. And you must strive to relinquish the bitter things of life, the poor things of life, for the greater things of life - the light and the truth and the love of God, that they may walk with you in your every day. For a miracle is to give. It is to give of your love to someone who is in need, and who having received, and because of it, they are healed.

Jesus said, "It is better to give than to receive", and the receiver having received and been made whole, then goes on his way and gives to others. For that is the Law, and that is the way that the Law must work. For only in that way will you establish in your world the truth of God, the power of God, the spirit of God.

If and when that is established, you will be amazed to see the difference that transforms your world from the one of greed and violence to one of love, happiness, and plenty.

This then is your aim, this is what you are working towards. But you must firstly begin to sort out your own life, within yourself. You must become more assured of God, and the presence of God, and you must feel that love of God. For the closer you become to God, the greater is His love and the more of that miraculous power can be transferred from you to others in need. That is the whole point.

I want you to listen to these words. I want you to think about them. Think what a change can be made in you when you take that seed of faith with God's love. And it can change the lives of others.

God bless you, and farewell.

THE TABERNACLE LIES WITHIN MAN

I greet you beloved in the name of love, and in the name of Him whom I call Lord and Master. About His business this day I have come. God Bless you.

It seems to me that many centuries have passed since that fruitful hour when my colleagues and I journeyed to a small place called Bethlehem, and there in a most humble abode, a stable no less, we found a small child who was, and still is, the Lord Most High.

It is difficult sometimes, when I glance back over time itself, to comprehend all that has happened. When I think of all the wonders that this small child, growing up to manhood, had accomplished, it is most difficult to understand fully how the world at large today could have grown so far away from Him in every respect, both in ignorance and in evil.

I know that if today, you were going to visit one of those far lands where starvation, death and disease are ripe upon the tree of misery, and to that land where there is war that is so terrible that it defies description, terror and fear are very much alive in the hearts of those who dwell there. If you where to go there, my children, and ask a simple question like "What do you consider to be the greatest gift that man could possess?", I have no doubt that the people would say to you "Peace of mind", for that is without price, and in no way can it be bought in the market places of the world. Above all else, nothing can bring to you that contentment that peace can.

You are here this day - a beautiful day that God has given to you, when the sun shines bright and the sky is blue, and you have few troubles but think you have many. You do not know how blessed you are, and in spite of all these blessings you have one additional thing, and that is the knowledge of God. You have that seed of truth within you that bears the hallmark of salvation, not only you, but as many as you will impart it to.

The alternative my children, is to fall into that pit of disaster, fear and starvation, which has befallen those very sorrowful nations far from this land.

Consider what I have said to you, consider it well. For here you have a treasure that cannot in any way be purchased by anyone in the world. You are blessed with the time that lies before you, spanning out across the years that are yet to come, and you have nothing in your minds as to what you will do with tomorrow, least of all the years that may lay ahead.

Yet you have the substance with you of a spiritual power with which to mould the tools of service to mankind, and to benefit yourself that your life may not lie idle in the bright lights and the glamour of your world, or in the unfulfilled desires within you, to become another rich person. All this is dross my children, is like fools gold. It is worthless, and hence it is worthless to your life.

Does your life mean anything to you at all? If it does, then WAKE UP and see clearly the way that lies ahead, and be thankful for what has been given to you by Him who is Lord of all. Trusting to you those seeds of a new harvest, to be raised up in the minds of little children, and men and women, so that you may bring to them that eternal water that once you drink of, you thirst no more.

Having received such gifts, I would like to help you to see their value, for truly it is clear to me that you do not. Truly it is clear to me that they still lie hidden, and the will to fulfill your own personal desire is still with you. That, my children, is death, and not salvation.

The will of God must be with you, it must be within your every thought to enhance every breath that you take, and every word that you utter. You have already touched upon the magic of God. You barely understand the Spirit of God. I in my humble way try to stir you from your slumber, that you may see for yourselves what treasures you possess if you but know how to manipulate them.

Peace of mind my children, is linked with the will of God, and the will of God is the Law under which you live. I speak not of mans' law, which is of no account. I speak of the will of God, the Law of God - which, while you may not realise it, you still live under. You are still subject to that Law, whether you are aware of it or not, it matters little.

Many there are who believe that having received their punishment at the hands of the courts of the land, having fulfilled their debt to society, the slate has been wiped clean, but that is not so. For there is a higher court to which you are called to hear and to abide by, and that is the court of God, according to the Law of God. That Law, my children, is subject only to what God has deemed man to live under.

Following your feelings and your thoughts, ask yourself how much you love God, that in some way you may measure just how short you fall. Was there not someone in the Bible who was going to sacrifice his son to God? Consider that for a while, for such was his love for God that he was willing to give his own son in sacrifice. For he knew, that God in His love and compassion would take care of his son, and give Him a better life than he could give. It was not necessary, for God had tested him and found him not wanting.

I suppose that is a question we do not ask ourselves many times - how much do we love God? I suspect that we think that it does not matter very much, for after all, how can you measure love within you? Is there any instrument that is able to take its depth and its breadth, its height and its quality? Of course you are right, there is none, but then you see, love cannot be measured in that way. It is not like water, it is not like flour. It is like none of these things. It can only be measured by what you are prepared to give up for it.

What does it mean to you? Are you perhaps prepared to give up something in your life in order to say to God, "I love you". If there was a law that said to you that something was illegal, and yet you liked to do that, would you be prepared to give it up in order that you would be able to show God that you loved Him, and wished to follow His Laws? Or would the test be too great for you - would you fail. Would you not be able to accomplish that? None of us would know. Only you would know, for it is in you. It is not in anyone to measure the love that you have.

God demands of you that you give your very life into His hands, and this is why you are tested on many occasions, When those gathering clouds seem to blot out the very existence of the joy and happiness that you once had, When all things seem to be going against you, does it put greater exertion on you? Do you find it more difficult to go to your God in prayer? Yet that is the very time when you should go to Him in prayer, even though you feel empty inside and cannot fully comprehend what He wants from you, or even what He wants from you at all.

But your loving Father does this for you, not out of meanness, not out of hatred, not out of pleasing His own whims, for He knows that the only way for you to be strengthened and come to that more perfect way of thinking and loving, and respecting the gift of peace, is by bringing you face to face with pain and suffering. By testing your faith to see if you are weak, or if your love is strong.

You are not here in this life just to walk through it daily and do what you will. There is far more for you than this. The pleasures of life are always there, and how much of your time when compared to your pleasures, do you give to your Father God? How much of your time do you give to your brother who is in need? How much of your time do you give to those teachers and helpers from spirit who labour with you to unfold you as a servant of God, that you may be raised up in the true spirit of grace and light? All these questions you must ask yourself, for they belong to you.

Your Heavenly Father has said, MY TABERNACLE LIES WITHIN MAN. I shall wipe away all his tears, there shall be no more pain, no more suffering, no more death. They shall be my children, my sons, my daughters, and I shall be their God.

He speaks, when He says these words, of the time that is yet to be. In that time when all the darkness has cleared from the skies of man, and the misery that roams the face of the world because of the greed and the jealousy out of man. This is the time of which He speaks.

And so here we are, you and I, we sit and think and talk of both great and small things, little realising that such a time may not be so far away as you imagine. When in that time must be found in your mouths those electrifying words of truth and comfort, to be given to as many as will listen, for their salvation. In an unseen time and an unseen land, there they wait, to receive what you have to offer.

So perhaps you can imagine the importance of all these words that I have given to you, not just today, but all the yester-years, all the months, the weeks that have passed, and the very reason they were put in word-form on paper, given to you all to read and digest, read and digest, READ AND DIGEST, that they might dwell within you, that you might suddenly see the motive behind it all, and the power that motivates that motive. That you may know and not be found wanting for an answer when the question is raised - "Does God love us? How can He love us when we are in such dire need?". What will you say, my children? What will be your answer?

"Friend, tell me, is there a God above? Does He care about us?"

What will be your answer, my children? For you would have had to bear the same strokes and the pain of the same whip that has lashed their backs too. But will you be strong enough in yourself to say, "Be of good cheer my son. I tell you that your Father in Heaven loves you all, and in a little while you will see His mercy shining upon you. It will bring you salvation, and you will live in a land of milk and honey".

If you cannot believe that, you will not be saying it, for in those words must also be the power to rejuvenate their faith and strengthen their minds against their fears, doubts and hatreds. Yes, you will need all of this, you will need to have your love for God intact to give all that you have to Him, because you love Him.

Do you think to yourselves that He will be unmindful of you, or of all that you have striven to do, for I tell you that He will not. For in those times you will be blessed with that peace that passes all understanding, and that love that gives fulfillment and contentment to your soul. Think then to yourself, was it all worth it? I say yes it surely was, for to be the servant of Him who is my Master is beyond words for me to describe.

So my thoughts return to that time when as a child He lay in a stable, and my companions and I went to visit Him. there upon the hillside were the shepherds, tending their flocks, and the air was charged with that holy power. The angels of God said, "Peace on Earth and goodwill towards all men". That was the beginning and yet it was also the beginning of the end.

Lift up your faces, and feel humble that you have opportunities before you. Do not race hither and thither in search of this philosophy or that philosophy, for I have given you the truth and there is no more for you to know. Read what I have said, digest what I have said, and proclaim it as your own. Then it will not fail you.

So, with these words my children, I will take my leave of you, in the peace that you find and the love that you feel. If I have perhaps made one or two a little ashamed, then so be it, but I mean no harm - just to remind you in case you forget and are left behind. Farewell, farewell.

THE ANGELS ARE STILL SINGING....
(Christmas Message 1992)

I greet you beloved, in the name of the Lord Jesus, whose humble servant I am. Peace be with each and every one of you.

The reading that I chose this day is one selected to bring you the truth in Christ Jesus. For many in your world do not believe that Jesus was the Son of God. If you listened to the reading, you must realise that if Jesus was not the Son of God, then that reading was false and was never said, and did not happen. For only by being the Son of God could Jesus have done all the things that He accomplished. Perhaps above all, the wondrous teachings that He gave. Simple truths that were laid down as part of the Law for man to follow.

If you listened to the reading, you would have heard how it was prophesied over many, many years prior to the event, that a virgin would give birth to a son. Even in those days, such a thing was impossible, and yet, nonetheless, that prophecy was fulfilled.

When those words were spoken, all that time ago, those who were there to hear. listening to the prophet who gave them, believed that Jesus was about to be born. They went about their lives, looking for this child that was to be born of a virgin. I must tell you, that those who listened, questioned - What was this child? Why was He so special? And the prophet who gave them that prophecy enlightened their minds, as to one who was of the family of God, the Son of God. As to one who was a king. Whose name would be Emmanuel, meaning God with us.

When He came, He was to bring with Him a great and wondrous light, to serve the needy and to fulfill the will of His Father in bringing into being, and projecting into the minds of men, that Holy Spirit which is God.

I have no doubt that you who are here, and live in comparative luxury to those who lived in those days long ago, could not understand, could not see and feel, the joy that was in their hearts, believing that it was imminent, and that perhaps they would come face to face with this Son of God who was to shine like a Jewel in the heavens above.

But of course, you know what happened. They all passed away into that greater, fuller life, where they comprehend it all so much better. And yet the message that was given on that day lived in the hearts and minds of the people over all the centuries that were inbetween, filling some men with a great and wondrous glory, filling others with contempt that a man should even begin to believe that a virgin could give birth, and they laughed and scorned.

And yet, the belief that that would take place remained, in the hearts of many people. So you can see why it was that towards the end of that time, when that prophecy was to be fulfilled, how man had lost his faith. For he was under the heel of the oppressor.

There were many sick and diseased people, not only sick in the body, but in the mind also. Poverty was a constant companion to so many. So it was only to be expected that only the faithful few were still waiting for the fulfillment of God's promise. And what a promise it turned out to be.

That night when the child was born, was a very special night. One on which you had to be there to sense and feel the very change in the atmosphere. For all around you there seemed to be a great magic, a stillness that reached into your soul, and made you conscious of who you really were. It was indeed a wondrous night, for the very earth seemed to be tingling with the Spirit of God.

You know the events that followed. That Jesus grew to manhood, took up His ministry, and performed the works that none had ever done before, and none have ever done since. He spoke with a voice of authority that none ever did before, and none has ever since. For all those before, spoke: "The Lord thy God has said". But not Jesus. For He stood there, in the very power of God. He had that authority with Him, to change the commandments of God, and did so.

I suppose that few there are, who remember that it was also prophesied that this Jesus, Lord of all, one day was to return. And because He seems to tarry, they grow impatient, doubtful. It is easy for them to cast doubt upon the words of the scriptures, upon the words that were given. For that is all they had to build their faith upon. They had nothing else you see.

So to believe that Jesus was not the Son of God, but the son of man, and to believe that Jesus did not perform those miracles, as it was stated, but did no more than perhaps the average medium does today, was so easy for them. So easy to compare the events of today with the events of yesterday. And once they had rid themselves of the idea that Jesus was in some way special, born from a virgin, then the rest all fell into place. It was said that the people of that time elaborated - put it all out of proportion, and that really it did not happen that way, it happened just as it happens today, and no more.

But He stood with the Lord Most High in those days when He was ministering to the people of His time, leaving no doubts as to who He could be. For to stand in that Soul's presence, left you completely convinced. For such was the power that emanated from Him, that I have seen strong men weaken as they stood in that light.

At first they would attempt to challenge and heckle Him, yet later they fell upon their knees. For when you stood in that presence, you soon became so conscious of who this man was, and who you were. It did not matter whether you were a disbeliever, that you had never believed that there was a creator, a God in heaven or any where else for that matter. It didn't matter. But when He brought you into the circumference of His power, all the other things that were dark within you fell away, and there you were, naked before your Maker. Naked as a child before its parents. Naked, because they could no longer hide their sins, because they could no longer deny who this man was. Naked because of the shame that had gripped their hearts and minds, through all that they had done. And I have seen them my children, confess before Him and cry like a baby, with tears streaming down their faces "Lord, Lord, forgive me, for I did not know it was you".

And it seemed that in that moment of time, all the events of their past spirit life before they were born, were laid open before them, and they knew Him. Not inasmuch as you would say His name is this or that, but there was that oneness with Him in your soul, and you were conscious of that help you had received in the past tense.

"Lord, Lord, forgive me, for I did not know it was you". Think of these words my children. Coming from a strong man whose ways were far from gentle, and who had always been harsh and violent.

When He looked at them and put His hand on their heads and said, "Arise, go your way and sin no more". How could they have even guessed what depth of love and compassion this man had? That He would forgive them all their sins.

So you will see and understand, my children, that to us who were in His presence constantly, there could be no shadow of doubt as to who He was. We knew the kind of power that was with Him, that there was nothing in this world or in the universe at large that would not obey a command from Him.

We did not truly understand everything, because it was beyond our power of reasoning. We could not comprehend the magic of it all. We Just knew that it was there, and we loved to be in His presence. We could not bear to be away from Him.

Many peoples' lives were touched by Him. You have heard only recently, I believe, from one who found Him nailed to the cross by His side. There were many, many such events that took place in individual lives, so that it would be impossible for me to tell you their stories too, but I hope that over the time that is left to us here, we will be able to use some of them, to bring you to the greater feeling of truth.

Many, as I have said, bowed down before Him in shame, but there were those who had wonderful joy within their hearts, because they had believed and knew that this event was to happen. Such as the blind beggar, who knew He was passing by. He knew, as he knew that all things with Him were possible.

"Lord, Son of David, heal me!" And those who stood by said to him, "Hush. Be quiet"' But he cried the louder. "Lord, Son of David, heal me:" And Jesus heard him, and said to him, "What is it that you would have me do for you?"

"Lord, that you should give me my sight".

"Then let it be according to your faith".

Instantly, the blind beggar was blind no more, but could see all. Tell me a man, be it in your time, or be it in another, who has performed such miracles as this. Tell me his name, I beg you. For I have never found one.

I suppose my children, that I was greatly blessed in those days. Little did I realise, when I was a crown prince and destined to be next on the throne in Persia, that I would become a humble peasant, serving the Master, willingly give up all that I owned, that I might become a humble servant.

And now, Christmas is here my children, and the angels are still singing. Still declaring, "Peace on Earth and goodwill towards all men".

Who will listen? Who will listen to the greatest gift that God could give man? They have not done so, so far. We still find a darkness within the minds of men. We still find him persuing his own enjoyment and pleasure, knowing not what it might bring him. For whatever misery it can cause him here, I tell you greater misery lies ahead, when he makes the change called death.

And you who sit here! Do you hear my words and believe them? Or do you hear them, and tomorrow they are gone, lost on the ether, having not found a resting place in your hearts?

You, who I have said, the Lord knows you. Have I not said to you, ten thousand might fall on your right side, and ten thousand at your left, but it shall not come unto you? You are those to whom I have said these words. You are those to whom I have said that I have come from the Master's side, and He gives me the permission to bless you all with His love, and says that He loves you so deeply. You are these, my children, whom I have laboured with so long, and so well. Do you hear my words, when I tell you? Or do you in secret, perform the will of Satan? Do you? Only you know. You and I, and Him who is my Master. Only we know. We shall keep your secret. We shall not reveal you.

It has been said, that Jesus will come again, for when He went into Heaven, and left His disciples gazing upwards, two angels said, "Ye men of Galilee! Why stand you here, gazing into heaven after Jesus? Know ye not that He will return again in the same manner as He went?"

Those in olden times were told, "A virgin shall give birth to a son, and His name shall be Emmanuel", That came to pass. I see no reason why the return of Jesus should not come to pass also, and perhaps time being what it is, that time shall not be too far away, and you, my children, might witness that coming, and be able to judge for yourselves, when you stand in His presence, whether I did you an injustice when I told you of the strong men who were brought to their knees by His love. You will be able to judge, and it is my prayer to the Holy Father, that it shall not be your shame that brings you to your knees, but the joy of standing in His presence.

The greatest gift that you can give to anyone at Christmas, is your love. Wrap in up in that very special paper called love,- and send it to God asking that He may bless them.

If it is your will, YOUR WILL, you will feel the presence of Christ in your homes. But remember, it has to be OUR WILL. It would be beautiful if I could think that sometime over the Christmas period, you my children, might find your feet leading you to church. Not a spiritualist church, but a Christian church, going perhaps to a candlelight service, or to Christmas carols. It does not matter what is being said, you understand, but rather the presence that is there, that you can feel and sense and take it to yourselves as being that you were close to the Lord Most High.

And so my little ones, although I must say farewell to each one, I want you to know that I will be with you on Christmas Day, and I want you to be aware of my presence and to feel that I am there. For you are to me like my chicks, that I watch over. Through all your trials and tribulations, we have brought you through. Perhaps not in the way that you expected, but we have brought you through. And so shall it be for evermore.

When I come again, I shall give you the teaching that I had intended to give today, but because it was voiced by one among you that they prefer a Christmas address, I changed it. I hope that you found something in it that has inspired you, and lifted you up to receive that fair portion of the Spirit of Christmas.

Farewell. God bless you all.

TRUE DEDICATION
Plus questions and answers.

Good afternoon and God bless you, my children.

What is true dedication? When you come here and sit for your development, you may not be totally aware of those souls who have journeyed back here from the realms of light, to inspire you and to direct your thoughts, filling you with that new purpose of spirit and that greatness of God's love.

True dedication means that no matter how hard or difficult the task may be, you must devote that day or time to being there. That is the whole importance of the thing. You cannot in any way, turn up after the circle has started and expect to be let in. If a time is stated for you to be here, then you must be here at that time. Anything else in your life which may intervene in that time, must come second, for your whole purpose is being in your seat when the time comes for you to be at one with those who travel back from the realms of light.

I stress the realms of light, because I want to show you how much more difficult it is for those who are your guides and teachers to be here with you. How much they have given up, how they take on these new conditions that are harsh and cause them suffering, in order to be with you. If they then, can do all this without a measure of pain to themselves, then surely you can make that effort to be here with them.

That is all I wish to say upon the matter, for I realise that there are those who should be here but are not, and of course I realise that there are those who are not here but they have valid reason.

So my children, what shall we speak of today? It is not always easy to find a new subject when part of your circle is absent, at a time when you should be giving to them a teaching that was due to be delivered on that day. For it means that if given, then they have missed it, and it is always important that nothing is missed and that your presence is here.

Seeing then that I am not able to speak on the matter that I had come to deliver, I have now to find something to speak to you of. Perhaps it would be a good idea to review the time that has passed, and the things that we have discussed on previous occasions, and to give you the opportunity of finding an answer to those things that were perhaps not too clear to you at the time of delivery.

So, if any of you have a question that you would like to ask, upon whatever matter that is of a spiritual nature, then please go ahead and do so. I will answer to the best of my ability.

Q: Could I ask you a question about the spirit world - the different levels with the spirit world. Also, we are all individual spirits, so are all spirits created at the same time or are new spirits being created all the time? Are spirits actually disappearing as well?

A: When you say disappearing, what do you mean?

Q: I mean that they have created such evil, that they no longer exist.

A: Yes, that is so. To give you a precise picture of the spirit world and its different levels is perhaps asking for the impossible, for after all is said and done, you must achieve a new spiritual height of understanding that would allow you to pass from one light into a greater light.

That is the difference between one sphere and another.

If you are travelling higher, you must realise that the new Sphere is brighter in every way, because it embraces a great deal more of God and truth and love, and as a child cannot come from the infants and go straight into the senior school and be expected to understand what is going on, and why it is going on, so then is it in the spirit, where one may pass from a lower into a higher level, and find themselves at peace with all around them.

For if they were not in unison with that light and with that greater glory, they could not enter. It would be a barrier to them, for the same maximum and quality of light must be in them, in order for them to blend into the higher realm through which they pass, in order that the new realm may be made manifest to them, and that they may be able to see all the things which are there for them to see. Had they not been capable of reaching that dimension, then the light would be such that they would be blind to all that was in it. Do I make myself understood?

And so, if I were to ask you, what is necessary for you to pass from one sphere to another, I would say that the quality of the soul must be enriched.

It is not a question of sitting for an exam, and if you pass the exam then you continue on. Nothing that is added to your soul which enriches its quality can be spoken in words, for it is not in word form. It is the quality of love, the quality of goodness, the quality of sincerity and the quality of Godliness within you, and they are not in word form. They are very real, and have a substance of their own, a substance which enriches your soul, so much so that you are able to pass from one realm to another, and comprehend all that you will find in that new realm.

There are many such realms to which you progress. None of them can be acquired or accomplished within a short space of time, for within the realms in which you find yourself there are many different facets of experience and vibrations, and different kinds of learning that you must come to see and understand. Many things which at first you will not understand, you will not comprehend.

It is true to say that you will go to school in the early part of your spiritual life, and there are teachers there who will instruct you. But they do not use a blackboard and easel, they do not write sums on the board, they do not give you history lessons. It is nothing to do with that kind of learning, but it is rather a soul-searching lesson to be learned about yourself. Coming to terms with yourself, and coming to terms with your life, to see if you are able to put together and see the things that were wrong and were directly attributed to you, so that you may pass by that basic level of coming to know why you are as you are. Once you have accomplished this, it gives you a new insight of what your goal is to be, and how you are to accomplish that goal.

It is not easy. It is very difficult, for the learning of that has to be in experience. When you have drained everything from your life that you can, through the experience of that life, and there is no more for you to learn from, then you must go on to tackle new concepts of spiritual life, in order for you to understand more clearly the things that you are to evolve to.

Many are these things of which I speak, you have no knowledge of. No one has ever taught you them. Nobody can speak of them for they are those unspeakable things without shape or form in your world, or according to your understanding, and yet they are there.

The universe is not just a pretty thing that is hung out at night for man to look at and say, "Oh, isn't it beautiful". For well he knows of all the planets and stars that exist there, but such a very small grain of sand compared to the mighty desert of truth and knowledge that there is to be gathered.

There are new depths of the soul that you must delve into and conquer, and you can only do this when you are brought to the knowledge of their existence, and you must feel your way with yourself, in order to find them. You must be placed in situations that challenge you, challenge the old values that you once lived by here on earth, to see how strong they still are within you. To see what depth and trust and love you hold to God, by being in that position where there is fear about you.

A great deal of the early work is done in the lower regions, where you are sent to help establish a greater depth of truth within them there, to help them rise above the pit that they are in. But that is not the only work. There is work that is afar off, across the other side of the universe in other forms of life and to other forms of life, and yet all part of the creation of God.

There is so much there that I cannot speak of because there are no words that describe. It makes me feel most inadequate as your teacher, but this is the only way I can explain it except to say that one day you will experience these things for yourself. You will come to know just what I mean, for we are all in search of God, but who is God, and where is God?

Each one has a vague idea within his mind, but I am afraid that that is nowhere near the truth. Mans' conception of God is totally wrong. He sees Him as a figurehead. A great power and like a fatherly figure, but that is not so. For you are totally reversed around. Maybe that is an odd word to use - reversed, but it is the only one I could use to show you that you are now looking in a direction of God and all that God is, in a most ineffective way. When you do come to realise that you are in search of God, and who God is, you will see why there is still so much before you in order to reach out to that great spirit, that great Father of all His children.

It is not a simple thing to comprehend and understand, even I at the level that I am at, do not know what God is. I have drawn a lot closer to Him, and I have been able to see totally differently to what you see, and understand totally differently, but I do not know what God is. God is more than a word, indeed WE are more than a word, we are Gods in miniature.

To understand what your quest is, you must begin to understand yourself first, and in order to separate the imperfect and the perfect within yourself, you must see how utterly useless the imperfect is, because it blinds you to the truth. It prevents you from going any further. It is necessary to cleanse oneself, to cleanse your mind and your spirit of all that which is imperfect, and that is a tall order, a very tall order.

Consider for yourself, that if you who sit here now do not even understand what perfection is, in the state of mind and the condition that you are presently in, then what will you understand of that condition on a higher level of thought and a more clear image of yourself?

You begin to see the obvious and cleanse yourself from them, and as you go on and cleanse yourself from the obvious, then you begin to see other imperfections in yourself. Other things that you need cleanse yourself from, which are more deep rooted than the obvious.

And so it goes on, and the purification is taking place all time. When you stand before a greater light than yourself, then those imperfections cause you great pain and anguish, and perhaps the hardest to rid yourself of, is the thought that you are a lot better than you really are.

So you see, as much as I would like to be able to paint a clearer picture of the question, I am afraid that that is as close as I can come. Do you understand?

Q: Yes, thank you.

A: Is there anything else that you would ask?

Q: Yes. Those people who are on Earth at the moment, have they come from different stages of spirit?

A: Yes.

Q: Is it possible for someone to come to Earth to regress so that they may actually have come from a fairly high sphere, but they can in fact get lower, and vice versa?

A: Yes, even angels fall from grace, and if angels can do that then it is most likely that man will. Oh yes, that is so.

Q: So are angels of a higher level of spirit?

A: Angels are a different creation to man. They are, how can I say, nearer to the Godhead, whereas man is a child of God and one day must be as God is. But we are a long, long way from that, and the higher you progress, the more you are able to see the distance that lies between you and that goal that you must aim for.

So the answer is, that angels are and always have been on a different level from what we are - they are not those who are born into the world. They have no need of that. You must then ask what of this guardian angel that you have often spoken of?

There are such guardian angels, but they are men who have progressed to a much higher level of spirituality, and you are placed in their charge while you are here on Earth. Not to interfere with your free will, but to give you the understanding of God, the knowledge of God at one stage of your life, and that by so doing, you then may choose the path by which you choose to walk. Is that understood?

Q: Yes, thank you. I would like to know why sometimes you feel as if you are alone, and you know you are not alone. Why do you have that feeling?

A: It is also part of your test if you like, for all these things are meant to give you an experience of different feelings. Surely you will feel at one stage of your progression, that while you feel alone, it is then that you need to summon all your strength and faith in God. To maintain that spiritual light that you think you have, or you think you feel. It is when that cloak of protection is taken from you, and you stand alone, what you do in that period of time is very essential to your progression, and your overcoming of difficulties in your spiritual progression when you come to us.

Loneliness is one of the things that you will experience, in order to overcome that feeling of being alone, to create the within you to bring to yourself the knowledge in the true state, that nobody is ever alone. No matter where you are, or how you feel, God is always there.

Any more questions? You seem to be a fairly knowledgeable group of people, or I seem to have been a great teacher! All the things that I have said need no interpretation or answers in your minds?

Q: Can you tell us something about moods? Why is it that sometimes we can wake up and we are in a certain jolly mood, or an unhappy mood for no apparent reason?

A: Are you speaking primarily of waking from sleep, or the moods that can change during the course of the day?
Q: Both really.
A: A lot of your moods stem from your health, for if you could trace body's health, if the body is feeling tired, listless, or in pain, then your mood will change and you will feel that mood. But not always is a mood one that will depress or depleat you. For many times a mood can be one of joy, if something has been said to you which surprises you and gives you an inner feeling of 'glowing with pleasure', or 'I am pleased' it changes your attitude and your outlook in certain ways, and brings to you that feeling of joy.

There are other ways in which moods can change. Bad dreams can cause this, and they are usually based on the events of your life, and linger in your subconscious, coming together because something in the day has sparked that thought off.

In that dream it can be very frightening, very confusing. So much so, that when you wake, you wake in a very unhappy state. A depressed state. So moods are subject to varying conditions of life, and your health, and also your sleep state. But you can wake up having had a good dream, feeling on top of the world. Moods are very funny, because they can be changed from one moment to another. What can be so happy in one hour, can change to a source of tears in another, but that is basically all that you can say about the moods of people. They are formed and created out of the substance of life.
Q: How is it that some people dream, and others don't?
A: All people dream. It is just that some do not remember.
Q: Why is it that we do not remember?
A: That is a difficult question. One that I do not feel capable of answering, and I am certain that whatever I could say about that, would probably not be right. I cannot really answer that question.
Q: Are all dreams from the subconscious, or have they any form of substance?
A: Most dreams are from the subconscious. There are others that are related to travel in spirit. Some of these can foretell the

future, but at the same time I would not recommend that you place all your faith in what you have dreamed, regardless of how real it may seem.
Q: On this Earth we have quite a lot of different races and colours. When we seem to be so much at war over colour, when the soul passes over into spirit, I believe that all souls who are of an equal level go to the same sphere. Does that also mean that those who have been fighting over race or religion all pass to the same level as everyone else, or are they separate?
A: Man will find his level in the world of spirit according to the spiritual light that is within him. You cannot go beyond that light. You must rise or fall according to your works. Therefore, if they have been of an evil design, then they will fall to the level of darkness. If they have been of a spiritual design, so they will rise to that spiritual realm of light which is in keeping with their souls. Does that answer your question?
Q: Yes, thank you. The animal kingdom, are they in a different sphere to us, or are they with us?
A: It can be so. There is no difference in that respect. Although I want you to know that there are certain parts of your sphere which does not have animals, not because they are barred, but because it is not suitable for them. An animal has its own sphere, and its own progression.
Q: Did you hold the doctrine of the atonement - that is, that Jesus, by his death on the cross, atoned for the sins of mankind?
A: At an after period of my life I held and preached doctrines somewhat similar to those held by Paul, but now I have changed my views of the doctrine in question. It is not alone by the death of Jesus, but by his whole life on earth, that man can be benefited, and by taking him as their great exemplar. If men would follow him - that is, love their fellows and love their God (for he did all that), then most assuredly, when they pass away from the mortal body, they will be admitted to the blest mansions of the Just. I believe that Paul would now tell you the same thing.

Now I will say farewell, and God bless you all.

BREAKING THE LAW AND ITS REPERCUSSIONS

Beloved, let your hearts be still that they may be touched by the peace of God. Let your minds be quiet, that that noise which troubles you, from the worries of your life, may be driven away. For we come to speak to you softly and yet compellingly. Softly because it is the word of life that we are imparting to you. You gather here in a oneness to be closer to your God, yet how quickly the memory of it all flies from you when you leave to go about your daily business.

As well you know, it has always been our intention to bring your souls alive to the knowledge of Christ. He who is our Lord. Well you know that it has never been our intention to raise you up as mediums, for always we have said that we are striving to raise you up as ambassadors for Christ, that you may carry that potent word of truth into the lives of all men. Because we are striving to raise you up in this way of discipleship, much more is needed from you. For you must learn to embrace the whole of God's Law, and make it your own. If you live one fraction outside that Law, then you will never he a child of God.

God has said that He will come and live amongst you. You will be His people, you will be His children - His sons and daughters. To be this then, is to depart from the frailties of the human form. To lift your minds to that purity of God where you are bound to the Christ Spirit, for it is that Christ Spirit that must be raised up within you as it was in Jesus, fulfilling every aspect of your life.

Your body must be in the world at large, but it does not mean to say that either your minds or your souls must sojourn in that life. To live under carnal law is as dog eats dog, and if that is what you want, then best you go and serve the master who holds that law over mankind. For you are the servant of him whom you say you serve, for saying and doing are two different things. So you serve the master whose will you do.

When you perform those acts within the world that please you, little do you understand what lies ahead. Little can you see of what the future brings. Take the gardener who plants the seed, he knows what is going to be raised up, and he will cultivate his land accordingly so that the seed might be given every opportunity to thrive and succeed in life. But if you plough and you sow according to the wild side of nature that grows in the wilderness, then only that will spring up which you have sown.

Because there has been no planning, no proper preparation, then it is a rather haphazard affair, Just like nature that is wild. If you go into the jungle it is impenetrable. So then, exactly the same thing occurs when you sow the wrong seed in your life. Well we understand why you do this, for it is some kind of attraction to you. It fulfills some kind of joy, but the reverse is true. It is even more so, if you knew what the truth of it is.

You are children who have left your home and travelled to a strange land, and have been given no memory of life that was before your birth. Therefore, it is easy to see why all the things of this world please you, because you are living a different form of nature to the one that you have left. In that life, only the fulfillment of peace and happiness, and the joy of loving God and being free, was your aim. You understand also, that if you ever were to depart from that Law, then those things could no longer be true.

Even if you go back to the beginning and read the story of Adam and Eve, there in that time when they dwelt in that wonderful land, by breaking the command of God they fell from grace, and were born into the world. It was not. God's punishment to .them, it was the Law that they had broken, As you cannot walk into fire without being burned, so too can you not break the Law WITHOUT ITS REPERCUSSIONS. I want you to realise that very emphatically. By showing you the story of Adam and Eve, I think that you can see it, even though I say to you that the story of Adam and Eve is to this end, fictional. It only in some way shows to you how the beginning of mankind and his troubles came into being.

They lived in a golden age, in paradise, and they broke that commandment, and that is what led them here. Because it did, they had to learn why they cannot live in paradise if they wished to accept life under another law. It is the law that you live under now that troubles me at times, for all of you have work to do, and that work must not in any way be marred by the absence of that true purity of God.

You are His disciples. If this is what you say you are, then this is how you must live your lives. You must see and understand the difference between carnal man and spiritual man, and realise that carnal man shall surely pass away when the end of the world for him comes. That is to say the day that he dies, that is the end of the world for him. The spiritual man must be raised up. But if the spiritual man is not spiritual, then the place that he abounds in is in the darker realms.

To change the thinking of people, you must be as good as your word. I feel, my children, that you are as good as your words when you know God. When you feel God, and the presence of God.

Many people say you cannot see God. It is because they use the wrong eyes. For God is only seen with the eyes of the spirit, and you must learn to exercise those eyes here and now. They are the spiritual eyes - that which you feel. Unless you exercise them, then they will never grow to that point where it becomes a second sight to you.

Go into your woods, your fields, and all around you is God. You can feel, and through the feeling see what God is. Understand what God is. He is everything that grows around you. He is everything that is beautiful there. He is every good thought that you ever had. He is the mighty oak, the blade of grass, the daisy, the butterfly, the bee, the leaf on the tree.

His power gives them life, and what you see is the mind of God. He has laid it bare for you to see - the mind of God with all its beauty. You gather to yourself its strength, its peace, and you ask yourself, how can I become part of that feeling of God?

You are already part of God, for His life is in you, and He wants to sustain that life in a pleasing and peaceful way. One that is without violence, one that is without hatred, without desires that inflict damage and pain to others, one that does not fill itself with greed, one that does not only think of itself, but of others.

If you go into the woods, into the fields, you will see all around you those things that harmonise with each other, and give to each other, as a tree gives a home to the birds, and to many other forms of life - insects - life and food. They blend in with that Law of God that keeps them in harmony and not at war with each other.

Look at the flowers that you have before you. They have been in the mind of God. They were designed and created and given life by the mind of God. Is there an ugly one among them? Do you see them fighting for a superior place? Do you see them talking about their neighbour? Do you find deceit there with them? Do you find them filled with a kind of grievance that creates unhappiness? Does one shine above another? God gave them the same right and the same beauty, and He has given that to you. It is for you to use it rightly.

When you think of the gifts of the spirit, what do you think of? Healing, clairvoyance, prophecy, teaching? But do you not understand the many gifts that God has given you? The image that you are, and you look at other peoples' faces but you do not see them wearing your face. You are you. You are unique.

What else has He given to you? Fair hair, a pleasant smile, sparkling eyes, a musical laugh, a soft voice, a gentle touch, a humble nature, These are all gifts too, that God has given.

He has given to one the ear for music - he writes it down and plays it, and it gives pleasure to others. They listen, they are inspired, and for a little while they are beyond this realm, in the realm where perhaps angels dance.

He gives to another the gift of painting. Of capturing on canvas the beauty of a tree, or the face of a loved one, or the flight of a bird. This too gives great pleasure to others, who look at their work and think that there they have captured that moment in time. They have crystallised it, and it is there for ever.

To others, He has given the ability to play instruments. The piano, the violin, the cello. He has given them the gift of being able to play all in harmony, the same as His birds. Have you noticed, have you listened? When they sing their praises to God in evening song, thanking Him for the day and asking Him for protection for the night. Though there are many different birds singing in a variety of whistles, singing in different keys, yet from the humblest one who is just as sweet, to the most gifted one like the nightingale, they all are in harmony. Just like the instruments of a great orchestra. Harmony you see, my children, harmony.

Then there are those who have been given the gift of great voices, to sing, and each one has their own particular quality of voice. Each is defined by some tone that is different from others. It is also in harmony with the orchestra that plays, and you can sit and listen and find upliftment there. There are others too - architects who design and build great cities throughout the world. They also are not forgotten.

There are the mothers who give life to God's precious gift of a child. With special qualities to be a mother, watching over her charge to protect it, to nourish it, to keep it clean, and to feed the thoughts that it will think, into its mind. If they are harmonious thoughts, then happiness and joy will be its way. If they are thoughts lending themselves to spitefulness, and to jealousy and to hatred, then strife stands in its path, and bitterness in its mouth, and it loses the edge of all the good gifts that God has given. For it no longer knows how to be in harmony with all that is around it, for unless you are in harmony, how can you keep the Law of God? When you live outside the Laws of God, you are not in harmony any more.

You too have special gifts, that you can use. Gifts of the spirit, gifts of healing, gifts that bring comfort to the bereaved, teachers who unfold the mystery of life for man, to bring a deeper understanding to a mind that is confused. You can help them spin that web of harmony once again and give hope to those who have lost.

But it is what you do with your gift that matters, and like I have said, we are not raising you up to be mediums who serve the spirit, we are raising you up to be the ambassadors of Christ Jesus. Think what an honour that is, that you will go before other men and other women speak those words of Christ because you are His ambassadors, just as I do to you now, because I too am His ambassador. I too bring to you that word which will nourish your minds and your souls and enrich you with that spiritual yearning to be at one with your Lord.

I send you before the faces of the multitudes to speak His word of truth, to speak of His coming, to speak of His love, to speak of His holiness, and in every sad heart make joy spring up like the waters of life, refreshing every thought within their minds. That within every mind, that has been on fire with desire of the flesh, held prisoner by ignorance, may the chains fall away, and the gates of their prison spring open, that they may see the light of God's graciousness and say, "I was walking in the wrong direction all the time. That is where happiness lies, that is where my God lies".

For it is within you all, my children, the very seed of your soul knows your Father, and knows Him well. It is but to give that seed a chance to come to the will of God, and it shall hunger no more, neither shall it thirst any more for the ways of carnal man. Let peace be in your hearts, let your minds be ablaze with the truths of God. Let God be your lives.

I bid you farewell, farewell. God bless you.

If you ever read the Dead Sea Scrolls, you will realise how bitter they were against Jesus, and against Paul. You will see how they tried, through their lies and their hatred to bring His works to nought, and anyone who can read them and believe that such things took place, surely could never have read the scriptures and the works that He did. For never in those Dead Sea Scrolls will you find works there that are equal to what He did, and what He said.

He was the Master as it is written, and that which took place after His crucifixion was indeed the good news that went forth through many lands.

I know of no other man, no other prophet, whose works and words are still alive in this day and time. All those years ago, and they hold true today for you, to listen to and to weigh up the great truth that is there. That you must become established in that truth, and turn away from the things of the world, and the troubles of the world, and try with a loving heart to bring the light of that truth to mankind here and now.

It is very difficult, my children, and I tell you, it will never be easy. But you are not trying to capture the hearts and minds of all men, for no, not even Jesus could do that. But you are trying to serve those who are looking for the truth. Who will find a great restlessness with their souls and yet do not know what it is. You can bring that truth to them. Make their lives positive, enriching them with the wealth and treasure that God has given to you.

Farewell, Farewell.

THE TRUE MEANING OF FREEDOM

Reading: Luke 16 v 19-31.

There was a rich man who was clothed in purple and fine linen, and who feasted sumptuously every day. At his gate lay a poor man called Lazarus, full of sores, who desired to be fed with what fell from the rich man's table. Moreover the dogs came and licked his sores. The poor man died, and was carried by the angel to Abraham's bosom. The rich man also died, and was buried in Hades. Being in torment, he lifted up his eyes and saw Abraham afar off, and Lazarus in his bosom. He called out, "Father Abraham, have mercy upon me. Send

Lazarus to dip the end of his finger in water to cool my tongue, for I am in anguish in this flame". But Abraham said, "Son, remember that you have in your lifetime received good things, and Lazarus, in like manner, evil things. But now, he is comforted here. And besides all this, between us and you a great chasm has been fixed, in order that those who would pass from here to you may not be able, and none may cross from there to us". And he said, "Then I beg you Father, send him to my father's house, for I have five brothers - so that he may warn them, lest they also may come into this place of torment". But Abraham said, "They have Moses and the prophets, let them hear them". And he said, "No, Father Abraham, But if someone goes to them from the dead, they will repent". Abraham replied, "If they do not hear Moses and the prophets, neither will they be convinced if one from the dead should rise and return".

Here endeth the reading, and may God grant unto us an understanding of His word.

The True Meaning of Freedom

Good afternoon and God bless you, my children.

The Kingdom of Heaven is like a bright star. That which you can see and are travelling towards. The Kingdom of Heaven holds a great promise and mystery in the minds of men, and perhaps that promise is more important to those who have lived a life here which has been filled with tears and suffering. For they look for the time when they may be free from their suffering, and may go and live a life that is filled with joy and peace.

Perhaps not so to those who have all that they need here, and live in the lap of luxury. For after all is said and done, they have their pleasures and their joys that please them.

But, if you look around your world you can see for yourselves the unhappiness and the misery which is there, you must surely realise that that is man made. And over the course of time there has been much written about the misery of this world, and how it must surely fall away, unless man changes his attitude towards his brother.

Many have become slaves to their brother, and do his bidding, and they do all this, that they may receive a wage by which to live. It has never been right for any man to be the servant of another, and when I say servant, I am not speaking of spiritual service, but speaking of material labour, for that has always been where the problem begins. The problem begins with man subjugating his brother under his will, and he has never been given the right to do this, for all men are equal, and all men are free, for all men are a part of the great family of God.

While you who sit here know all these things, it is always a good thing to remind ourselves of what is right and what is wrong. Well you can see what is taking place in your world today. Well you can see how all this is coming into being because of man and his greed to rule. To rule in a place that no one has given him the authority to do, and out of it, you can go to every nation and see the end product. For the end product is never to the good of the people, only the good of the few. For when men rule they become greedy, and they exercise their authority in a secret way, hidden from the eyes of those whom they rule. Because they do, they take the bread from the mouth of the child in order to fill their own larders.

In that greed, their ignorance does not permit them to see what the outcome will eventually be. In that greed, they can never aspire beyond the point of thinking of self. And throughout the world, both in the governments of every nation, and in the powerful industries at large, they bond together in order to have that power to rule.

Now to rule, my children, in the way that they wish, is evil, and can in no way be acceptable to God. For only the rule of God, once it rules in the hearts and minds of men, can fashion a world that will give joy and pleasure to all His children.

Think about what you have, and what you need. Do not all these things come from God? Does He not supply them all? Oh, I realise that man must put in the work and the labour, to sow the seeds in the fields and to reap the raw materials of the Earth, that they may fashion them into the things that are needful for him, but that is where it goes wrong. For all these things are given freely by God. If it were not so, all your labours would be in vain, and you would accomplish nothing.

But because God creates and injects that power of living energy within every seed, and brings into being the very substance of Earth that man needs, and man lives, in his limited imagination, he wields the rod of authority and has created a society that is hemmed in on every side by rules and regulations, so that no man can live in this world except he apply himself to those rules and regulations, if he wishes to live.

Man has been robbed then of his freedom. Robbed of his labour, for what he received in payment is but a pittance. He works and accomplishes nothing, for it is gradually taken away from him in taxes and high prices. So he remains, in a sense, a slave to his master, and has to do his bidding, according to his task master's will.

I realise that you live in the world, and perhaps you do not see things this way. Perhaps you do. But this is the foundation upon which is built the moral fibres of mankind. This is what he is encouraged to accept as payment, in a world that seems to believe that if you pay them with the frailties of the human form, they are happy and content.

Like for example, the ways of man that are against the Laws of God. Prostitution and sexual relations without need of marriage, strong drink and drugs. All seem to be part of their plan to satisfy the need of man that he does not look any higher than his own selfish desires that lay within him, giving him no scope to come to that crystal clear thought of what is righteous and true, and what is of God, and who they should be.

Not only is all this there to hold mankind in his place, but also those who dictate the ways of the world - in who should eat and who should not eat. Who should die in wars, and who should live. For those who embark on such things as wars never go themselves. They always send their slaves to do their fighting and their bidding.

You may not see yourselves in this way. You may think this is not true, this is not right, but when you think about it in a more logical way, you will see that it is perfectly right.

If one should raise up his voice against the establishment of man, then he is quickly removed. If one should preach according to the ways of God and seems to be heard, then he is quickly removed. There is always one waiting in the wings, waiting to assassinate. You have seen this so many times.

So it is small wonder then, that God cannot in any way accept this established world that man has made. For it is in no way acceptable according to His Laws. For they have corrupted the minds of His children, they forbid the truth of God to be spoken to His children, and for why? Because to do so brings them down. So God is unacceptable to them, and the Laws of God are unacceptable to them, because they oppose everything that those Laws stand for.

If the Good Shepherd should come and stand once more in the cities of this world, crying out against the evils of this time, he too would find an assassin's bullet waiting.

So now my children, when you see all that has taken place in your world, the corruption, the evil, the hungry, the diseased, the dying, because you see all this and cannot deny it, because it is there, you cannot say that it isn't, you must surely realise that if that world is to come into being as God promised, where He has said that the meek shall inherit the Earth, and that He will dwell with His children and He will be their God, and they will be His children. If this is to take place, then an almighty change must come into your world, and the very establishment and its foundations must crumble. For almost now, that era must begin to be born. A change that wipes away the evils of the old, and brings into being that new world upon which the spirit of Christ inherits. Gone must be the old hates and prejudices exist here now between the white and the black, and the Jews and the Germans, and all other nations who have hatred against another, like the war you have now in Yugoslavia. For all these have been incited within man in order to have control over their minds, and their lives.

Man must always think, and he must think for himself. Not which comes from a philosophy that comes from greed and jealousy, and hate, but free to think about what is right, and how to live your lives. To rid themselves of all those evils that bring misery to them and in no way makes them spiritual souls. Gone must be those whose religious thoughts cannot aspire beyond that point which is the boundary of their own religion. Those who say, "If you do not believe as we believe, then you will go to hell". For they too harbour great hatred and ignorance, and they are the children of ignorance who divide man against man and allow the evils of suffering to go on.

Out of the truth is born the knowledge that God is love. Out of your hearts, in compassion, is born the knowledge that God is love, and love is joy, and joy is happiness, and happiness is contentment. All these things together are your life.

We look therefore to the day, when one's labour does not belong to oneself, but belongs to one's neighbour, as well. We look to the day when the Law of God is imprinted upon the minds of all men and they, in turn, live accordingly, and bring into this world that beauty, that majesty, that is of God.

If I could this day take you all back with me into that great world of spirit, you would be full of wonder. You would never want to come back here, and you would see just how you are living your life, and the things that are wrong with it.

YOU WOULD TRULY KNOW THE MEANING OF FREEDOM. You would truly know the meaning of happiness, for it would be in your soul, bubbling up like a mountain stream that refreshes the weary traveller.

You would see there such beauty and such marvels that you would never have thought possible. No night follows day there. No weariness follows toil, no enforcement of labour because you have needs that you must purchase from another, for every day is YOUR day. Every day is a day of joy. There are no dark clouds waiting to appear on the horizon because you suddenly think that this holiday is finished and you must get back to the grind of life.

And the things which would fill your mind here, no longer do there. Things like what will you wear and what will you eat. What will you do and where will you go to have your pleasure. For the least things on your mind are the clothes that you will wear or what food you will eat, or where you will go to have your pleasure, for such things no longer exist.

What DOES exist, is that joy that comes from the spirit within. Fashions for you new thoughts of life, and being where your contentment is not based on where you will go to find entertainment, but comes from knowing that you are a child of God, and that nothing pleases you more than to give service to Him and your brothers.

There is a great wealth of love that flows from you, one to the other. Even the smallest thought that is not in keeping with love is very painful to you. When you perhaps meet those whom you have known in life, and perhaps have not always dealt with kindly, there are many tears and much remorse, as you beg their pardon. For you can see and you can understand far better in that new environment than ever you can here, where you are shut away in an environment that is filled with danger, filled with tears, filled with grief.

We do not wish that for you, but like soldiers we prepare you, and we give you the tools that you will require to smash down this regime that will not give freedom to man.

Are there any questions that you wish to ask?

Q: We seem to be talking about revolution.

A: Totally.

Q: Will God start this revolution, or are you saying that we should be starting it?

A: You have already started it. You started it when you accepted God and the love of God and the Law of God to live by. It is not a revolution where a man fights his brother to the death.

Your weapons are not weapons of destruction, but weapons of truth that destroys strongholds where lies are concealed. Your weapon is the weapon of truth, and the sword of truth that slays the unjust, and brings to all that knowledge that they really thirst for.

You must first of all be able to show them, that they may be able to see in their hearts and minds, that vision of a new life, a new existence. Not the one they have now, for it is full of cares, worries, and doubts, but a new existence which is based on God's Law. And when you can penetrate their minds with this, revealing to them a vision that is free from the tyranny of man and his hates and petty greeds, which will revitalise them with a newness of life according to Christ Jesus, then you will begin to stir up the courage and spirit of people to fight with you.

This will come. Inevitably it will come, whether it is forty, fifty years from now. It will come, for that regime which is in existence here denies the truth of God, and will not allow the Laws of God to be in operation. It is sinful in many ways, and that is the regime that will fall, and is already at this moment of time in which I speak, crumbling at the foundations.

God has ALREADY set His plan in motion. No man can see and no man can prevent it. It WILL be done. The work WILL be done.

Q: Will there be tremendous anarchy whilst we switch from this regime to the Law of God?

A: No. Because man has yet to come to see the misery that this way of living is to bring him. How can the meek inherit the Earth except they pass through the valley of shadows? Once man has done so, then he is meek, because his fears are beginning to live a terrible existence again.

Even you, my children, do not realise the terror that is there, but will one day wake to its reality. BEHOLD I MAKE ALL THINGS NEW. And so it shall be. If you must make the change, when you pass from this world - from the existence that you know now, to the one that you will know - and the difference is so striking and so easy to accept and embrace

(Except for those who hanker after what they have left), then men shall not find it any more difficult than making that change from one to the other.
Q: Will you talk to us about the work that you are expecting us to do? Is it more than just teaching?
A: When a child falls over, do you walk by it or do you pick it up? Do you not know The answer? It is as simple as that. As obvious as that.
Q: As obvious as that... There is nothing that we are not yet aware of?
A: Nothing that I have not told you. Many things which will happen - you cannot foresee and are unaware of, but that does not mean to say that you will not see the rights and wrongs of things, and what must be said and done.

Even now, you see, as 1ong as you linger and do not heed the word of the Lord and come to His side, then of course you spurn the work that He has for you to do. The quicker that you hasten to His side, then the better it is for the work that you must do.

You need to speak and you need to be brave in your speech, and YOU MUST SPEAK WHAT IS TRUTH. For only the truth can set you free, and only the truth can give you the courage to speak.
Q: And yet you have said that we should be careful whom we speak in front of...
A: Do not cast your pearls before swine I have said.
Q: What would you say then, that we wait for those who appear to have an interest?
A: Always those who look for the truth will draw that truth from you. You will know those who do not want to know, who do not believe and would make a mockery of what you say - you know those. There is something about them. Something about their speech, something about their attitude. They are not the ones who pick up a small child. They lack the compassion and they lack that urgency to help others, for they think only of themselves.

To them, your words are like pearls cast before swine, for they will use your words against you. But for the many who sit even now, because they know that there is a greater truth and cannot find it, cannot bear it, do not know the man who knows, when you meet them you will know them also.

Q: And will God see to it that some of them will cross our paths? Because otherwise, how do we find them?

A: They will cross your paths every day. Perhaps you are unaware of them, but they are there, and this is the sensitivity that makes you aware of the presence of those who are searching for God.

It is in the gentleness of their voice, and in the words that they choose. In their attitude. It is there. And so when the opportunity is given, you plant the seeds of goodwill and truth within them.

That seed will be raised up and bloom, and the truth will be born within them. They will find their way to God. They then will find their way through the scriptures that have been given, by seeing with new eyes and understanding, having a clear mind, not one that is confused.

It will happen more and more, day by day, week by week, month by month, year by year, as you go on from this point. It is not written in vain that the Lord will come again. I tell you that you are very foolish indeed if you do not believe that to be true, for surely it will be so.

When Jesus stood before Pontius Pilate, and He was asked if He was a king, He said, "Not of this kingdom. For if it was of this kingdom, then my armies could fight for me, and they are legions strong". And when He returns again, those armies that are legions strong will be with Him.

Remember that Jesus said, that in the latter days many would come saying, "Christ is here, and Christ is there". Believe them not, for when He comes, it will be as a thief in the night. So if one should came and say that they are Christ, believe them not. Christ has not come yet, and when He does, you will know.

Q: Will it be before all things are made new that He comes?

A: Oh before, yes.

Q: Is it anything like in Italy, where people are sick of corruption? Is it a change like that, where people turn round and ...its very marked...

A: Oh yes. Oh most definitely. Where people will begin to see the wonders of God. That is when they need people to teach them.

Q: Because that is when people turn to religion, isn't it? When they've had enough.

A: Yes, but do not forget that I have also said that religion is corrupt as well.

Q: Yes, O.K., but I do not mean religion for the sake of religion, but they return to God.

A: Yes, I know what you mean, and you see that the reasons that has all to be changed is in order that when they turn and accept God, it must not be according to little minds who have hemmed themselves in because they believe they are the chosen ones. They are not the chosen ones. None of you are chosen.

Q: I mean the ordinary people turning to God.

A: Yes, that is right. They must receive the truth, and when that corruption begins to show itself even more than it does now, then you will find that there is such an outcry that there will be an almighty change. But in the transformation there has indeed to be, a lot of suffering which cannot be avoided.

Q: Are you talking about our country alone, or on a world level?

A: In the world at large.

Q: Are you talking about natural disasters, or because of the sudden awareness of corruption?

A: Natural disasters have happened. Natural disasters will again happen. But there are disasters that are not natural because they are made by man, and he is poisoning the very Earth upon which he lives.

Q: Are we to have more nuclear spillage then?

A: Nuclear spillage does not necessarily have to come from the power plants which generate your electricity, for already that radiation is coming from the sun because of the hole that appears in the sky AND WILL CAUSE DEVASTATION. But the greed of man will not allow him to see it until it is too late.

You cannot oppose the will of God. You cannot. For the Law of God is wholesome and whole, and when you oppose it, it means that there is corruption and weakness within that which you oppose it with. That is like a cancer that destroys the body, and you are the host of that body, the body that you call Earth. The body supplies you with food and your life. To oppose the Law of God, is to bring devastation upon the Earth. There can be no other way.

It is like me saying to you, tonight instead of darkness falling, you are going to see the sunrise. You know that is not right, and neither can it be right when you oppose the Law of God. For when you do so, then you have let a chink come into the armour. You have cracked it. You have made it weak, and you have brought in the evils that come with that new law of self that is there. That is what has happened. Now this is the whole problem. Man has been told this over the centuries by all the prophets, by the holy men. They have been told all of this.

Q: Can I ask you, what is it that has caused the destruction of the ozone layer, because if it is C.F.C's, that was not a wilful disobeying of God's Law, it was accidental.

A: It was also a destructive element, because when man discovered it and had a chance to repair it, he did nothing.

Q: So it IS C.F.C's then?

A: Oh yes. It is all kinds of things, which is the way that man is.

Q: And the bomb? Splitting the atom?

A: All of this is part of the decaying world in which you live. All the poisons which you feed to the vegetables and whatever... the sewage even that is pumped into the sea. The waste that comes from the nuclear power stations. It is all part of the decay that is happening.

Before that happened here, the decay started in the minds of men. The decay comes from his MIND, from his thoughts and his desires. He gives preference to the frailties of the human form, and allows them to rule him rather than to be ruled by the power of God, and the love of God.

The love of God is a great healing balm which if allowed, will be expressed through man, and because it is, it heals oth-

ers, because it takes away the pain and suffering into which others fall. Because that love is compassion, which creates the need to help them, and therefore it is a healing balm. It heals, and it heals Mother Earth, and nature. It is all these things.
Q: It is an evolutionary thing rather than an individual thing, isn't it, because some people cant help the way that they are behaving, because they have been conditioned.
A: That's right. Young people have been conditioned, not by what is right, but by what is wrong, in order that those who have this great yen to rule, may rule, and rule according to their own ways, not according to God's.
Q: So we are looking at the evolution of the Earth, rather than the evolution of the individual soul...
A: The individual soul has its own individual evolution, that is being touched an prevented by the plan of man, and it prevents that freedom of spirit and the freedom of thought, because it has taken away from him. The opportunity is not there.

I am sorry my children, I must leave you now. God bless each and every one of you.

Farewell.

FROM LITTLE ACORNS, MIGHTY OAKS ARE GROWN

I greet you beloved in the name of love, and in the name of Him whom I call Lord and Master. Peace be with each and every one of you.

My children, because of the events that have taken place over the last few weeks, which I am sure have been sad for all of you, where one of our members no longer resides here in the physical body, but has come back to her spiritual home.

(The person referred to was Ivy, the beloved wife of Douglas Arnold). And reassuring all of you that she is here present today, and I am certain that she will make that presence known and felt to each one of you, it did however seem to me that perhaps I have need to speak to you about the passing from this life to the life that is to come.

For you all know that when you pass from here, you are going to enter into a world that is totally different from the one that you have. In many ways it is far more beautiful than the one in which you live, for all the harshness that you find here in life is no longer with you. Neither are the pains of the physical body, or the doubts and fears, worries and troubles of your life. They cease to be.

But what you also carry with you into that new environment, is a great deal of what you enjoy in this world, and that becomes something of a handicap to you, in the beginning.

Of course the dearest thing that you leave behind in this world is always your loved ones. Well I know that you can see why it is that those who are left, grieve, and find it difficult to adjust their life without that very special person who has filled their life. But perhaps what you do not see, and do not always realise, is the same grief is felt by the one who has passed into the higher life.

For it is said, that as you are, so shall you be, and love knows no boundaries. For if it is painful here, it will be painful there too. For the separation between one whom they love, is no different from the one who is left behind. They too grieve, and grieve for some time. If that love is deep, and there is a real bond between those whom they left on Earth and themselves, then it is bound to be so. For love, my children, demands it be so. You cannot in any way change that law of love. It is in operation on both sides of the veil that separates you from eternal life.

So if you have been carrying any misunderstandings about this, I want you now to know. And of course all of this has been prompted by the passing of our sister Ivy, who is happy in every way, except that like my son, she too grieves for him, and longs to be with him, just as he longs to be with her. It is a natural state of affairs, one which should be so, for that is what love is. It binds you in that way.

Now our sister Ivy knows only too well, that my son must journey on for a little longer, even as all of you are aware of this, in order that the work should be completed. And if love is true, it in no way mellows, no ways dies away. It is only strengthened. And you will find that your sister, who helped so many of you here, will continue to do this. You will find her in your homes, and in your daily lives, as she makes her presence felt, and it will be felt by all of you. She is a very determined lady, with a strong will, and because of this, she is a very good helper. Already, most of you here have experiences to tell about your sister whom you knew, and who has come back to you and made her presence known.

She is going to take a very active part in this circle, and much more than this, for it is to be that you are going to experience a more physical phenomenon than you have ever done in your circle before. She is going to be the link, the missing link between us and that creation power for a physical demonstration as we have told you in the past, would take place. However, that is not yet. It is a little ways down the road, but it is going to happen.

Our sister has first to overcome her grief, and has also to settle down in her new home and find herself, then we will be able to gradually bring into being those conditions that we need. Quite contrary to what most people think about physical circles, the one that we develop, that we are striving for, is a spiritual, physical circle. In other words, it is going to be on a high level.

I am not going to say too much about it at this time, except to say that we have already on one occasion, given you a demonstration of how it is going to be run, realising that when it happened to you last time, none of you saw it. None of you, although you did capture it on film, and you have all seen it on film, even though lot of you supposed it to be something to do with the sun's rays shinning on the camera lens, but it was not, and evidence of this is that it only happened on one occasion, whereas your camera had stood in that same position week after week, with the sunlight shinning through the window, and yet there was nothing. Nothing whatsoever. So that must warrant some thought from you, to consider that if this is caused by rays of sunlight, why oh why did it never happen again? - why did it never happen before? For it is the same sun that was shinning through the window for most of your Saturdays during the summer when you met. And if you can see there something of a physical thing, which is of a spiritual nature, you will have some idea of what we are trying to do, that through the colours, you may see the spirit forms that build.

I have always said to you, especially to the older members of the circle who go back many, many years with us, that that day is approaching, and is surely going to be so, and we are close to it. And you will find that when things are ready to begin, you will not have to wait for the camera to reveal them to you as before.

I know that many of you here would dearly love to see that which we have spoken of regarding the Christmas tree for the spirit children, and who is to say that is not going to be also? I would dearly like to see that come into being. Not this year, not this Christmas, but let us put an extra effort to try to bring it into being for next Christmas, where we can also allow the spirit children to come and take the toys off the tree, and play with them.

Thus is our aim, but not solely this, for these are the things that we want to bring into being, to bring you more in line with the knowledge that God exists. For well I know you would all say to me, "But I DO believe". But, my children, not as firmly and solidly as you would think it so. We wish for it to be concrete. That you KNOW that God exists. And by this method shall you see and know, and when that happens, then you will see what I speak of. Why it happens. That by so doing, it will inspire all of you to work with a great zeal to accomplish that truth, and establish that truth in the minds of men.

Now you can see the other half, the other half of the story that is coming into being, of all those teachings that have been given to you over the years. Did you think that they were yours alone? Oh no. You are those souls who are to make it all possible. To bring and create into this circle of yours, those conditions of love and unity that are essential for us to come and deliver them to you. There could have been no other way.

In the minds of you all, you carry those seeds. You perhaps, at times, are not aware of what you DO carry. But all that has been said, has not just been spoken into the air, and then gone, but has found root in your minds and your souls. It has elevated you to more spiritual souls than you were before. More conscious of what you should be doing in your lives.

Consider then, all of this, for it has been the framework that has been built over those years. The framework that has been built in you to lay the foundation. The foundation which is to be raised up in truth, and therefore the message that has gone forth, and all the teachings that have been given, have now got to be spread throughout the world. Not just on this small island on which you live. No, much further than this, for in the world today, there are many souls who are looking for an answer. Goodly souls. Souls who cannot come to terms with the present day religions. And yet, dwelling inside them is an awareness that there is something greater. It is a longing to have that fulfilled in their lives. Where they will be able to know their God much more than they could ever come to understand in this life, in other religions.

And while, in the beginning of all this, things will seem to be a little confused, a little uncertain, you will find that little by little, it will all unravel, and the means and the know how and the wherefores will have all straightened themselves out, and soon you will be inundated with a demand to know more.

With all of this, there is a building set aside which will become your church. But it is not tomorrow or next month, it is a little way down the road. You are working towards it, and there is much to be done and overcome before it can happen. But it will happen if you are prepared to put your shoulders to the wheel, and work for that single aim of bringing all this into being.

And so my children, as much as I would like to stay longer with you, I cannot. I must not impose myself too much upon my son. So I will take my leave of you, requesting that you ask for inspiration from those to you from the other side of life. Receive the blessing of Christ, receive the blessings of those who love you dearly from our side of life, and receive the love of your sister who is here in a different body today (Douglas Arnold's wife, Ivy).

Farewell, farewell, God bless you all.

IN ANSWER TO A CALL

Good afternoon and God bless you my children. I greet you in the name of Him whom I call Lord and Master. Peace be with each and every one of you.

I come in answer to a call, for a question has been asked. As far as possible I will answer that question, even though my choice of words will only give you a measure of the truth that lies behind the question.

Well you know that I am here controlling this physical body, (Douglas Arnold), and well also you know that while you are able me speak you cannot see me, unless of course I choose to allow that.

So it would seem then, that spirit returning to this world, is not seen and cannot be touched by you unless they wish it so. But in the life that is to come for you, in the world from which I come, those who dwell there are as solid as you, and all things around are as solid as here, because everything is on the same vibration. A vibration which is much faster than the one in which you live, which is slower and coarser, hence the physical form here is much more dense and much more solid.

Now, many people reject the idea of a virgin birth, for they say that Jesus was no more than a medium, and there are many such as Him in the world today. But of course they do not see or understand the truth, or understand the law that is in operation through God.

If Jesus was just an ordinary man, then that would have made the virgin birth quite unnecessary, for He would have been a mortal man, like yourselves - physical in every way. But in this particular instance, where Jesus came for a very special reason, a virgin birth was very necessary, for He was born into the world as the Son of God. For Joseph was a man, and the spirit which dwelt within Jesus as a very high personage, and because He needed to do the kind of miracles that He did, the flesh that was born upon His body was not the same as that which is upon you. True to say it was solid and touchable, but the spiritual power which passed through Him was great, and the body itself was nowhere near as course as yours, and was always on a higher vibration. A kind of vibration that lay between this world and the one that you will go to. These things were possible because, with God, all things are possible.

Hence the reason why He could do such miracles as walking on water, telling the storm to cease, raising the dead, curing the sick instantly, and teaching with authority as no other man had ever taught. For there was no other prophet or holy man who ever existed who had the authority to change one of the laws of God, like Jesus.

He gave you a new commandment, and in so doing broke an old one, which said, 'Hitherto you have heard - an eye for an eye and a tooth for a tooth, but a new commandment I give to you, that ye love one another even as I have loved you'. That word love came into it perhaps more than it had ever been allowed to come into the lives of men before, mainly because men in the older days could not accept a law such as that. And when Jesus gave you that law, He pledged you all under the law of love, which incorporated every commandment that was ever given you - that ye love one another.

Now, when Jesus was crucified, His body not being the same as yours, was indeed taken into Heaven, and it happened in a very mysterious way. For little do people realise that the wife of Pontius Pilate was a follower of Jesus, without her husband even suspecting. It was she and her servants who took the body of Jesus out of the tomb because she feared what would happen, not realising that she had no need to do so, because the body would dematerialise of its own accord. For the body of Jesus was never found and never will be, because it was never here in the form which you are here. Had He been here in your form, He would have had to obey the laws that govern the physical body. But His body was under a new set of laws, a set of laws which were laid down by His Father.

That was the reason why His body dematerialised, and was the reason why He appeared to His disciples in solid form, not like the materialisation of spirit which is done with ectoplasm and cannot be touched. His body was totally different, and he walked with them and talked with them, even sat down and ate with them, after His crucifixion.

It had to be this way. It was a holy power that was in Him, and if only man could stop and see the reason why the virgin birth had to be so, then he would be able to comprehend a great deal more of what took place.

Of course you are privileged to understand a great deal more than they do. You have been given the essence of that truth, and it is for you to use it whenever the subject should arise.

Now you have heard, wherever it is written in the scriptures, how Jesus took bread and broke it, took fish and broke it, and gave this to five thousand people. Where do you think the extra food came from? Do you think that He was a magician? Someone who had a magic wand?

No, Jesus was using the law of God. The law that said that God is the creator of all thing, and He is able to supply your needs, as He did at that time for those people. The multitudes that were around Jesus, He was able to supply their needs.

It was in accordance with God's law, God's spiritual law. For how do you suppose that nature provides you with all your food if it is not given by God? If it is not from God, then pray tell me where it comes from. Scientists cannot produce it. Scientists cannot make one little seed that produces a flower. But God can, For He does not only supply the seed, He supplies the fruit of the seed, and the power within it to let it grow and prosper in that way.

So my children, for as much as the question was asked so I have given an explanation, and of course when Jesus comes again - as He will, then it will be in the spirit, not in the flesh. He will not be born as the children of men are born, and grow to manhood. He will come in the spirit. And yet that spirit will be as solid as the one he wore all those years ago when He was with His disciples.

This is the reason why, He said to you, "If you had faith such as a mustard seed, you could tell the mountain to be cast into the sea and would obey you", because that is not the quality of faith that you have. Many of you believe you have faith, but you are not able to do the things which Jesus did, because it would not be possible to pass that power through you. You are too course, you are too solid. It would be outside of the natural spiritual law that provides and makes possible all those things that He was able to do.

As on the occasion when He was with His disciples, and the crowd grew angry and surged forward to stone Him. What did He do? All you read in the scriptures is that He 'passed among them'. What does that mean? It means that He had the ability to transport Himself (teleport), to another place. Once again, the evidence that He was not in a physical body like you and I.

His power was all embracing. There was nothing which, had He wished, He could not do. So you see, while there are many who claim Him to be an ordinary medium like themselves, I have yet to see any of THEM raise the dead or walk on water: Yet all you will get from them as an answer, is simply 'He never did those things, they are impossible to do'. For them yes they are impossible. For Him, no.

Man lives under a law. The material law. What one man can do, all men can do. But that which is beyond man, comes from God. So that is what I want you to see and understand. You must also take into consideration events that happened long after His death, relating to the Virgin Mary. For Mary has appeared many times over the centuries, and is still doing so today. In as much as she does this, she has performed miracles. Lourdes was one instance, Medjugorie (Yugoslavia), was another. And what do we say about such things? Do we bury our heads in the sand and say it isn't happening when there have been thousands of witnesses! Do you dismiss such things by saying they have all been mass hypnotised? I do not think so, my children. I do not think you can throw off the evidence of all of this, just like that. In particular, the events that have taken place in Yugoslavia, and which indeed will continue to take place for some little time yet. They are miracles that man cannot reproduce in any way at all. It is no use saying they did not happen, there are too many witnesses to say that they DID.

So they must continue to wander through life with their eyes closed, and their minds only open in one direction. The reality and the truth of it, is as I have said to you. Be it that you believe it or not, is entirely up to you. But one day when you have made that change called death, you will see it for yourself. You will see it in operation. The law of God does not prevail here, but it does in those higher realms.

One day, that same law will be fulfilled here in this world too, for it is said in the Lord's Prayer, 'Our Father which art in heaven, hallowed be Thy name. Thy kingdom come, Thy will be done on Earth, as is in Heaven'. And so shall it be.

Again, when Jesus said, "Blessed are the meek, for they shall inherit the Earth". That too, shall come into being, and that time is not as far away as man seems to think. Unfortunately, there will be a great deal more pain and suffering before that comes into operation. But come, it will.

Have you any questions to ask me on that subject?

Q: Was Mary chosen as Jesus' mother before she was born?

A: Yes, before she was born. All of that took place a long, long time ago, in the kingdom of Heaven. They were never souls that were like yourselves, they were all highly evolved souls. As I have said to you, many there are who do not need to come to Earth, but do so only to perform a specific task for God. When that task is done, then they will go on their way back home. Any further questions?

Q: Purely as a matter of interest, at what point was the body of Jesus removed by Pontius Pilate's wife? Did the body dematerialise after she removed it?

A: Yes. It was dematerialised before they had a chance to bury it. When they found nothing but the shroud they were completely lost for words. Lost for understanding. The shroud was then returned to the empty tomb.

Q: May I ask a further question? The shroud which is called the holy shroud of Turin - it did show impressions which I have always assumed were made at that moment when the body dematerialised - the energy force imprinting itself on the cloth.

A: That is quite right, even though your scientists seem to agree that it is not. The marks were made by the very power that Jesus was MADE OF.

Q: So the Turin shroud IS the genuine article?

A: It surely is, in spite of what they say. That doesn't matter. You must realise that a lot of these things that go on, like - planting the staff of some of those prophets and wise men, which turned into a bush, or flowers, even such as this - and they are still there - you can still see them to this day. Even these have not been accepted by man, and it was never meant for him to accept it. Only those children of God, the believers in God. They could, for it was in them to do so, but for others, it was just something to be ridiculed.

Had science proved that the shroud was in fact genuine, then a great weight of truth would have been revealed to man, and that altogether would not have been good. For why do you suppose that God has given you free will? It is so that you may come to the knowledge of God and serve Him from love. You choose Him from love. Had He proved that He had existed, He would have taken away the progression from many, many who did not believe, to such a point that they could not say that He does not exist any more, and they would have had to follow Him, not out of love, but out of the evidence that was weighted against them. It is necessary that man chooses God through love of God, and that is the only way that he can do so.

Q: At the Last Supper, when it was said that Jesus broke bread and implied that this was His flesh they were eating, and drank wine implying that this was His blood, did this in fact happen? Because there seems to be such controversy. People are asking questions as to whether He did in fact initiate that ritual. They seem to think it is a cannibalistic thing to do, that stems from the Druids at a much earlier date. How true is it. Did Christ actually do that?

A: Jesus did indeed sit at the Last Supper, and did indeed break bread and give it to His disciples, and did indeed say those words, but perhaps there has been read into it much more than was really there. I think the meaning was altogether different, the bread being the bread of life, and the wine being the wine of life. When He did this it was to say to them, "Whenever you break bread or drink wine, do it in remembrance of Me". But I do not think it had all the other bits and pieces which have since been attached to it.

Q: Am I right in believing that when Judas betrayed Jesus, that was his goal in life. It had to be. It was meant to be?

A: Yes.

Q: What happened to Judas after he passed over? Was he forgiven?

A: Yes, that is the simple answer, because it was for Judas to lead Jesus to His death. It was planned. Everything that happened there had to happen, and that was put into Judas's mind. He did not do it with any hate. He did it because he thought that Jesus would be able to get Himself out of it. Judas thought he would take this money and give it to the poor - that was his intention. But of course, it was not God's intention. Jesus knew, Jesus said to him, "Whatever thou.hast to do, do thou quickly", because He knew.

Q: Did he feel great guilt when he passed over?

A: He felt great guilt BEFORE he passed over, for he committed suicide. But of course, once he arrived on the other side, he was consoled by the answers that were given to him - that he was chosen to do that, and without him doing that and those events coming into being, Jesus would probably have been forgotten a long time ago. 1t was all part of the great plan.

Any further questions? No? then I will take my leave of you.

Farewell and God bless you all.

GOD HAS NO RELIGION
(Christmas message 1993)

I greet you beloved in the name of love, and in the name of Him whom I call Lord and Master. Peace be with each and every one of you.

I want today to be a day of joy for you, that your hearts may be lifted up and sense the Spirit of Christ here amongst you, for such is the Spirit which is here.

As I know you are aware, it is written that unless you become as little children, you cannot enter your Father's house. It is good then, that I have gathered around me little children, who have learned, not the ways of the world, but the ways of the child. For the child seeks only for good, and practices the love of God, and over the course of time you and I have gathered together, and little by little, we have raised up within you that Spirit of Christ - that Spirit of meekness and gentleness, of love and humility, forgiveness, tolerance and understanding.

It has been a special weave, for that yarn has now been woven into your garb of humility, and although some of you have yet to reach out and come to a greater and fuller understanding, you all do possess the child-like manner of which I speak.

It seems sad to me that I have to speak about a child that brought to man so many gifts. Not gifts of the world, you understand, but gifts of the spirit, enhancing them in the beauty that is God, opening their minds to a life that is far beyond the reach of this world, and comforting them with that seed of truth that has borne fruit within them.

For I remember only too well that time when my companions and I were asked to go and pay homage to a child that had to be born. The gold, frankincense and the myrrh were from spirit, for they were passed through the flame of light, and we had no doubts in our minds as to the importance of the journey, no doubt at all.

Though we had royal blood within us, if one can call it that, we saw our task as being one of great honour, for we knew that this child was the Son of God. We understood how very necessary His coming was at that time.

In all humility we began our journey, not feeling as if we were kings or princes of the realm, but feeling more like beggars going to pay homage to a great king. A king who was far beyond us in every way.

So our journey began, and although we had many different experiences along the road, by the power and grace of God we overcame the robbers and thieves and the wild beasts, until we found ourselves in that land where the star appeared in the sky. Like as of magic, for that was the only way that it could be described.

We followed that star, and with each step our hearts became more joyful, for you see, even we did not know the course of events which were to come forth from this young child. Even we did not fully understand the path that He was going to lead man on. For we knew that such a soul as this had been prophesied to come, but what He was to do was something yet again that we did not fully understand. We could never have foreseen the events leading up to this great occasion, and it left us filled with great wonder in our minds.

Who was this young child, that God should have chosen us who were not of His people, nor of His faith, to pay homage to His Son? Who was this young child, that a star was born to guide our way? How could such a thing be done, and yet indeed it was. As it is written, so it was.

Who was this young child, that the angels of heaven should come and sing about His glory? Fear not, for in Bethlehem this day is born a young Saviour.

Peace on Earth and goodwill towards all men, was His message. Who was He then, that He should be held in such high regard? We pondered these questions as we approached the stable where He lay.

Needless to say, it was of some concern to us that all these wondrous things had been done, and accomplished, and. yet here in a stable was born one of the highest in all the realms of heaven.

When we entered, we realised that there was something very different about all of this. It was like taking a step into wonderland. It was filled with a kind of magic that puzzled the mind.

There was a great quietness that filled the air with such a noise. That seems to be a contradiction in terms, but it was so. There was a peace that hung all around, and a light that seemed to shine out of the crib where the child lay. His mother and His father were equally as puzzled as to why all these things had been done. As to why we, of all people, should have been called to come and worship Him.

Many who have read this story believe that it was that God had chosen three kings to come and pay homage to His Son who was the King of Heaven, but they missed the most important thing. They missed that truth which God was trying to reveal to man - THAT HE HAD NO RELIGION. He had no religion to give man, and that His Son was OF no religion, but the Son of God who had come to bring greater truth than they had ever known before.

For all through the history of man where religions have been raised up such as Buddhism, Hinduism, the Jewish faith, Islam and Christendom, all have borne great prophets and teachers but not with the intention of bringing into being a religion, as such. For that only divided men against each other, and did not free him as the truth it supposed to do.

Rather, it was to guide man along the pathway of life, revealing to him that by peace and love, and by living in harmony with his brother, then so would he find the life that he seeks to have, of joy and happiness and fulfillment, in the knowledge that God is his creator and his Father, and that we are all bound together in the family of God.

For that is what we are. We are all the family of God. And when you look at all these various teachings, you will discover that it is man who has added and taken away, and built walls around the truth that God has given in the simplest of forms.

That was never God's intention, hence why we found ourselves in the stable where Christ was born. Hence why we were not of His religion or race, and yet came to pay homage.

When Jesus grew up, it was very apparent that His teaching was going to be different from the one that His people knew when they were children. But it was a teaching with a great light, and all who looked upon it with a sincere heart would come to see what was being said.

Many thought that He was going to be a great leader, a General who would chase the Romans from their country, and were bitterly disappointed. For He came with a great truth, which was simple and yet beautiful to behold.

It was a truth that was of a different value to all that had been given before. It was based on SPIRITUAL value, and not on Earthly value, and because of this, so many could not understand and turned away from Him, because they said He was a madman, and who had given Him the authority to make new commandments, as indeed He did?

"Hither to, you have heard - an eye for an eye, and a tooth for a tooth", which was the old Mosaic Law. "Yet a new commandment I give unto you. That you love one another even as I have loved you". And all His teachings were based on love and forgiveness, even to the adultress who was going to be stoned. In their law they would have stoned her, but in the heart of Jesus, in the compassion of Himself, with a few simple words He prevented them from doing that.

Said He to them, "Then let he who is without sin cast the first stone", and they could not find one amongst them who had not sinned.

He asked, "Woman, where art thy accusers?", and she answered Him "There are none, Lord, they are gone".

Then spake Jesus, "Then neither do I accuse you. Go your way and sin no more".

Many times He would say, "Go your way and sin no more". For to sin was to live outside the Law of God, and from it would come only hardship and suffering.

This is why He said, "Sin no more". He tried to teach them about the values of spirit, and the love of God. He tried to say to them, that two sparrows were bought in the market place for a farthing, yet one did not fall to earth except your Father will know. "And you, my children, are worth more than many sparrows".

What a way to try to show people how much God loved them, for they did not understand. Perhaps it would have been better had He said to them - you are worth more than all the gold and silver and precious jewels in the king's palace. Then, maybe, they would have seen what a great love God had for them.

But it was A NEW SET OF VALUES that He was trying to give them, for He had only said, 'What should it profit a man to gain the whole world, and lose his very own soul?". Meaning to say, that the whole world lock, stock, and barrel, was not worth the soul of a man. So how could He tell them that God loved them more than all the precious jewels in the king's palace, which were worthless?

What they did not realise, was that the little sparrow was worth more than the whole world, lock, stock and barrel. Worth more, because it is divine. It has been created by God to beautify the world in which man lives.

And you are worth more than many sparrows, so consider the sum that you are worth, not in gold and silver, but in the value of many sparrows. Worth many, many worlds. So in all of this you can begin to see the teaching that was evolving, that was totally different from what man had been taught to understand - what man had been shown, to say nothing at all of the miracles that He had done.

Can you in any way understand the minds of those who lived in that time, trying to comprehend what He said, least of all His healing of the sick, the raising of the dead, walking on water and commanding the storm to cease.

Such things were beyond their understanding, and many of them were frightened because He exercised a power that they had never known before. Because He had many enemies in the church at that time, and you can understand why. If they allowed this man Jesus to continue, they would surely lose all their power, and that did not sit very well with them.

Into the temple He went, and turned out all the money changers, and those who sold and bartered. He said, "My Father's house should be called a house of prayer, and you have turned it into a den of thieves". They did not like that either, because through all the business transactions which were going on there, they gained a share of the money. It was to this end that they plotted against Him and took His life, and well you know how they crucified Him.

There were many enemies of Him and His followers during the course of His life, and during the course of what took place after His death.

EPILOGUE

With his NEW SET OF VALUES Hafed has not only explained in a logical and commonsense way, the inevitable consequences which face humanity if we continue to behave in a completely irresponsible manner towards the natural laws that govern the universe, but he shows us how we can, and indeed MUST change our ways and our thinking if we are to survive into the next century and beyond.

Slowly, mankind is coming to the realisation that hand in hand with many of the 'improvements' science can make to our daily lives, come a whole range of nightmare side-effects, and science which only a short time ago was hailed as the great saviour of modern man, is now seen in an ever increasing number of cases to be nothing of the kind. At best it gives us distorted values and artificial lifestyles, at worst it threatens us with complete and utter annihilation.

At the recent international conference held in Kyoto, Japan, to discuss the consequences of global warming - only one of the many urgent problems facing mankind, the richest nation on earth, the U.S.A., out of national self-interest, adopted an attitude of 'Blow you Jack, i'm O.K.' and made only token concessions. Normally the U.S.A. is anxious to take top position when it comes to world leadership, but NOT apparently when it affects their own very comfortable lifestyle.

The Americans more than anyone should be setting an example for others to follow. Their concessions were too little too late. The greed of the mega-rich industrial companies and international corporations, as well as the scientists and politicians in their pay, try to lull the general public into a false sense of security and wellbeing, in order to fill their own pockets with bigger and bigger profits, but the evidence of their folly is clear for all to see, and the dangerous game they play affects the whole of humanity.

Arrogantly men believe they can upset the balance of nature and turn their back on God, the Great Intelligence, the very source of all existence, but they are learning to their cost that without God you CAN only have a Godless world. As we are sowing, so shall we reap.

Humans must understand their true composition so that they can come to terms both with themselves and the world around them. They must understand that HERE AND NOW we are part spirit and not merely a mass of material molecules, and begin to live accordingly. The sooner we do this, the sooner will we get our distorted view of the facts into proper focus. We must learn to work WITH nature - not against it.

Let us become thinking and purposeful beings once again, and not the mindless morons that so-called civilisation would have us all turn into.

Regardless of nationality, religion or colour, let the peoples of the world unite to find that peace, harmony, and love that is so essential to the wellbeing of us all.

For the sake of our children and future generations we must succeed in establishing A NEW SET OF VALUES - our very existence depends upon it.

".... Thy will be done ON EARTH as it is in Heaven" must become a reality.

Ronald Wright

INDEX

Other books available from Revelation Press

HAFED a Prince of Persia

(Autobiography)

First printed	1875
1st modern reprint	1988
2nd reprint	1988
3rd reprint	1989
4th reprint	1996

HAFED & HERMES

(Volume 2, Hafed a Prince of Persia)

First printed	1875
1st modern reprint	1988
2nd reprint	1988
3rd reprint	1989
4th reprint	1996

WHAT DID GOD SAY?

First printed	1987
Reprinted	1996

JESUS the WHOLE story

First printed	1989
Reprinted	1996

FLESH - the great illusion

(Autobiography of Ronald Wright)

Printed	1990

Out of print

HAFED a Prince of Persia

(Autobiography) "Dead" for 2,000 years he relates his own life-story.

Every December Christians celebrate the birth of Jesus and remember the "Three Wise Men" who paid homage to the infant and presented him with gifts. The Bible also refers to these men as "Kings", but who in fact WERE these men and where they really come from?

For nearly 2,000 years these questions remained a mystery, but in 1869 a group of researchers investigating psychic phenomena conducted a seance with Glasgow medium David Duguid, and what resulted was to be one of the most dramatic and important spirit communications since the days of the Old Testament.

An entity claiming to be leader of the legendary "three" spoke to the group and wished to impart so much information that a total of one hundred "sittings" over the next four years were required. Notes were taken and published as a book in 1875, but all copies of the original having now virtually disappeared, a spirit "voice" instructed healer-author Ronald Wright to revive it, and this he did in 1987.

The book gives a fascinating glimpse into the life of ancient times, and reveals aspects of Christ's life not previously known, astonishing knowledge quite beyond the capacity of either David Duguid or anyone present at his seances.

THIS BOOK HAS TO RANK AS A CLASSIC OF ITS KIND.

REVIEWS OF THE ORIGINAL BOOK (1876)

'It has an interest for us greater than the contents of any other book outside the Holy Scriptures - All Christian ministers should make themselves acquainted with this book'

(Glasgow Christian News)

'Of the greatest importance - One of the most extraordinary works that has appeared in connection with Spiritualism'

(The Spiritual Magazine, London)

'Viewed simply as a work of imagination, literature has nothing to equal this marvellous narrative'

(Religio Philosophical Journal, Chicago)

Paperback £5-95
(Add £1 for postage etc)

HAFED & HERMES
(Autobiography)

(Hafed a Prince of Persia, Volume 2)

In this volume Hafed gives us not only a glimpse into that other world beyond the gave, but answers many questions which have puzzled people of the earth throughout history.

Hermes, a childhood friend and disciple of Jesus, also gives an account of life with the Master, and answers questions.

A book that takes all the fear out of 'death', and gives comfort to those who mourn their loved ones.

REVIEWS

'It is a most extraordinary book and deserves a very wide readership indeed - the description Hafed gives of his reception in the spirit world after his 'death' and his reunion with his loved ones is a very moving commentary on the possibilities that await all of us'.

(Greater World)

'Articulate and thoroughly absorbing'. 'Of particular interest is the question and answer section in the rear of the book. Well worth acquiring.'

(Psychic News)

'Containing descriptions of the spirit world, clarifications of events in Palestine after the Resurrection which make interesting reading'

(Two Worlds)

'Difficult to do it justice in a review'

(Unitarian Society for Psychical Studies)

Paperback £5-95
(Add £1 for postage etc)

What DID God Say?

By Ronald Wright

Not a book for the bigoted or narrow-minded... but those who seek true enlightenment.

Is the Bible really the infallible 'voice' of God? Are the creeds and dogmas of the Christian Church in direct conflict with the teachings of Jesus? What does the Bible really say about mediums and spiritualism? Is Jesus really God? Can priests forgive sins? Did Jesus really 'die' for our sins? Is man made in God's image? Are churches or priests really necessary?
The answers to all these questions are in the Bible, but they are NOT the ones given to the people by 'The Church'.

It is claimed that the Bible is still the world's number one 'best-selling' book and this may be so, but it is also the least understood book ever published.

In this small volume the author not only deals with the above questions, but also comments on many of the contradictions and absurdities contained in the Bible.

The author also gives helpful enlightenment on questions relating to some of the 'mysteries' - mysteries which can only be explained by someone possessing true spiritual awareness. A well-known Baptist minister, the late Rev. William R. Butler of Highbury, London, once said of the author, "He has been given spiritual insight not given to all".

REVIEW

'A drastic break with tradition' ...'Sounding like an exasperated cross between Alf Garnett and A.L. Rowse, Mr. Wright disparages the Bible's original scribes'... 'this fascinating volume'.

(London Evening Standard)

Paperback £3-50
(Add 50p for postage etc)

JESUS the WHOLE story

By Ronald Wright

There have been countless books about the life of Christ, but this one is different in that it accounts for those tantalising 'unknown' years **BEFORE** his ministry began, which, blended with a single narrative of the four Gospels, gives a more complete picture of Christ's life than has ever been attempted previously.

REVIEWS

'If someone (not a Christian) wanted to know about the life of Jesus, here is a very readable book which tells the story in an understandable way - Ideal for a Muslim, Buddhist, or Hindu who wanted some idea of what the Christian story is. This little book is not likely to be found on the bookshelves of a theologian - a good reason for reading it'.

(Churches Fellowship for Psychical Studies, Scotland)

'This fascinating book is well worth reading'....' The timeless appeal of the publication perfectly captures the atmosphere of the time in a way lacking in many other publications on the subject'.

(Psychic News)

'It deserves a place on any serious readers bookshelf'.

(Greater World)

'Gives a more complete picture of Christ's life than has ever been attempted previously'.

(Spiritual Gazette)

Paperback £5-95
(Add £1 for postage etc)